Chasin' Freedom

The Rough Side of the Mountain

I0414647

1 CURSE OF BLESSING

"Jehovah Jireh!! Jehovah Shalom!! Jehovah Rapha!! LET THY WILL BE DONE!!!"

My trembling voice raises with God's wrath and lowers with his many promises. The rhythm of the unforgiving, southern rain pounds out reckoning with the roar of heavens thunder as I cry out amidst my chanting and wailing of extraordinary supplications to the most high. I done been at it for what seems like a week's worth of suns, but I know'd it to only be a two. With fervor I beseeched him for thirty-five hours through undrying tears and faith to move ten mountains. But this thirty-sixth hour is not mine to beg but to give thanks for all he's done and for what he is about to do. The final hour is Gods, 'lay and leave' as mama use to say when things got too much to bear. The act of laying my burdens at my heavenly father's feet, leaving it for him to do with it what he may, is the final step in this transcendent tradition. The humid Louisiana summer heat has a mind of its own bringing flash floods and high winds without a moment's notice. But not this night. Tonight's symphony of annihilation is being carefully orchestrated by God himself. Is it a sign of an answered prayer or sounding disappointment that his child would seek him out with such a request. Either way, not for me to ponder, second-guessing is not a part of the 'lay and leave' way. I start to heave from the foul stench of baby excrement and curdled milk creeping through the floorboards but begin to question it as the source of my illness as I'm truly not myself. I got babies hollerin' for titty and older boys yearning for answers all broke down crying on the other side of my bedroom door. Such a small price to pay for what mama is doing; they'll thank me in the end. But they's be fine. They at the same place that brought me to the point where I am now. It's just they pleading to me and not God and after tonight, they's gone know the difference. My grannybabe always taught me to remember that we came from a special group of people and to teach my offspring the same. She instilled that we were saints with a spiritual connection with God, highly favored by the most high. Taught me just as her grandmother taught her back in our homeland,

'*Just about anything you falls to yo knees and prays fo' will be heard and answered by the Lord.*

You feel the need to have the Lord on your side from the smallest to the grandest thang, he gone show up! And when he shows up, you will know his power! Granting you all the desires of your heart, even when those desires aren't in line with what he may feel you need. Because the Lord will work it out with you before you hop on that Glory Train. So you be mighty careful and make solid sure you know what you be prayin' fo', 'cause remember chile..... The Lord answers prayers baby, we might not agree with how he does it, but he will answer.'

I had been raised to know that when I meditate and take my walk with God, I must be sure to go to him in gratitude, go giving thanks....never selfish. But here I am today, on my knees asking the Lord for the unthinkable. I'm coming to him ashamed, but unyielding, confident in my pledge but frightened of his reply. I come asking him to break one of his commandments, one I wouldn't even dare to compromise. Lord knows what's best for all, even when it comes with so much hurt and pain. As for me abandoning my little ones while in my spiritual closet pleading for intervention and peace, I'm praying he forgives me for that too.

"Daddy! Nooo!!!"

The shrieks of terror I hear from my eight children confirm the end is near as the front door opens slamming up against the rugged, wood wall with such force that the foundation shifts, followed by a muffled thud.

"MAMA! He dead! Daddy's dead!"

My eldest child Cecil yells while attempting to bust down the old but sturdy door leading to my sanctuary. I ceased the three-day prayer petition after lending ear to the hush that came over my room as well as my soul. In an instant the torrential rains came to a standstill and the forceful winds were transformed into a mere breeze. At that moment I knew it was done. I opened the door to my oldest boldly standing brandishing a strange look of complacency on his face clutching my husband's pocket watch. The welling tears only begin to fall as I step out of my spiritual realm and join the rest of my offspring in the front room to comfort their bereaved hearts. The children cried for their father, well the ones that could remember him, the others were crying from plain terror. I reminded my children that God doesn't make mistakes; even in death. I told them instead of crying, we need to pray they daddy into heaven. And that we did as Cecil led his siblings in hymns, prayers, and words of encouragement for their deceased father's soul. I had gone to Jehovah as humbly as I knew how and the Lord heard my cry. Was I prepared for his response? I may never know. But what I do know is from that day forward I understood what my elders meant when they would speak about being mindful of how we pray. For we know he will answer but unknown is the outcome.

2 MAH MAY

A tear trickles down my cheek as I watch Sheriff
Brown and his lynch mob marching up tha road
brandishing torches, weapons and nigga neckties.
Growing up colored in our parish aint changed
since I was a child. Negro families still survive off
of hard work and internal will power with nothing
to show for it but healed up whip marks serving as
constant reminders of how not to behave. But
every now and again something has to happen to
jog the memories of the uppity nigga white folk's
thinks that lives deep within every Negro and so
for that, we all must take note. Everyone in the
settlement was standing out trying to see who was
'bout to get dragged out they house this particular
night. I already knew, and the only thing I was
wondering was what had took them so long to get
here. Normally in Tipton County when white folk
thank us Negro's done harmed one of they own,
there's no peace until they find the guilty party and
if they can't find him, any stand-in will do, nigga
neckties are one size fits all.

"You Thomas boys come on out here, 'fo I sends
ol' Bubba in dere tuh drag yawls out!"

Sheriff Brown steady yelling in his thick southern drawl, barely able to contain Bubba as the rest of his mob round the path leading up to my porch with such a commotion.

As I look into my mind's eye, I see this play out before it even begins. I see more death and bloodshed than what originally brought the sheriff to my house. I see lives lost through life and lives lost through death. I see Sheriff Brown as a possessed man on a mission that has reached his destination. It's what I can't see that's sending chills down my spine. The hidden hatred and spite for anyone of color, murderer or not. I see destruction.

"Sheriff Brown, you nor Bubba is comin' up in my house. Now I'll send out who you wants but you ain't gone keep scarin' my chillin's with yo nigga nibblin' threats."

I advise the sheriff looking him square in the eye clearly upset at his lack of regard for my standing in the parish.

"I know a crime done been committed, but me and mine ain't had nuthin' to do with it!" I adamantly express to Brown and his killing crew.

This wasn't our fight and I wasn't about to allow him to make it so. I stand my ground watching Brown laugh it up with his mob as he taunts me with Bubba who anxiously awaits her command 'cause she knows it's coming at any moment. The more the men heckle and yell their obscenities the less control Sheriff Brown is having over the giant bitch. Bubba the Bear knows it's showtime and we are on her stage; this is what Bubba lives for. She is notoriously known for chasin' down and chompin' on niggas and tonight ain't no different. Bubba is a canine standing close to three feet tall tipping the scales at two hundred pounds. Some say part wolf, some say part hound but all agree she's total carnage. When the bear dog turned six months old Brown took Bubba to the local blacksmith and her God-given teeth replaced with hand-crafted metal dentures. The additions are called 'nigga nibblers' and are feared by locals in and around the surrounding parishes. Tipton County has three deputies to assist the Sheriff and his biddings with Bubba being the fourth and by far the most popular deputy hands down.

"Now May"

Sheriff Brown begins as he and his fourth deputy ease closer to the porch where I solidly stand my ground.

"You's one of the few coloreds I respect in this town bein' you been workin for Gov. Gifton all these years, but yo kin done killed a white man, one of my very good friends if I might add. Now bein I'm sheriff an' all, I's here to do a job and I's intends on doin' it! We's hangin' us some niggas tonight now send dem boys on out May, I don't wants no trouble!!"

The mob rally's around the sheriff's six-foot rail of a frame cheering waving nooses or rifles.

I knew my kinfolks kilt ol' man Claxton. But that was after he come and threatened to shoot Cecil where he stood. I tried to explain to Claxton my son's part in the situation and how he was used by his older kin, but Claxton wasn't trying to hear no parts of it. My deceased husband's nephews from Chicago came down south to stay for a spell. Since them boys was toddlin' everywhere they went, trouble seemed to follow. Now they grown they aint nuthin but two-bit charlatans and the truth aint in 'em. This particular visit my husband's nephews decided to pull one over on my neighbor Claxton by stealing one of his horses and staining the eggshell colored coat of the mare with ripe

boysenberries growing wild in the fields, leaving
the animal's hair an earthy shade of dirt brown.
The slicksters told Cecil to take the horse back to
the old man, selling it to him for only a few bits to
make sure Claxton would take the deal. The city
boys wanted to make an offer Claxton wouldn't
refuse and it wasn't just to make a couple of bits.
As slicksters the men kept money, even if it wasn't
theirs. This stunt today was for laughs. They loved
making fools out of the white man whenever they
could down here. They reminded us all how they
hated the south and said we were fools for staying
in such a god-awful place; but for some reason
they couldn't stay away for more than four months
at a time. Cecil sealed the deal and my nephews
were set to leave on the train tonight up north.
Before any of that could happen it began to rain
just as Claxton was hitchin' his new horse up to
plow. Once he realized he had been swindled, he
came for blood and wanted it from my baby.
Claxton was innocent, no doubt about it but the
one mistake he made was coming here by himself,
shoulda' waited on Sheriff Brown, theman woulda
had a fightn' chance.
My folks still determined to make that train
tonight, but may be headin' for a lynchin' instead.

"This is what I'm gonna do Sheriff, I'm gonna go
inside and tell them to give themselves up and face
the law, even gone send my chile as I know he

played some role in this mess and he knowd he was wrong. But Brown... don't hang my child! Don't touch one hair on his head! He ain't killed no man, he had nothin' to do with the murder of Claxton and nobody else. You lock him up, do what you gotta do but don't hurt my child, YOU UNDERSTANDS ME SHERIFF?!!"

I command, resting assured in knowing he would listen to me since he wouldn't be able to explain to Governor Gifton why he hung not only an innocent man, but a child of mine. I've worked for Gifton for close to thirty years. I grew up with his children being that my grannybabe worked there most of her life, playing a major role in the rearing of Gifton himself.

"Sheriff, you waits here..."

Before I can enter my meager abode my babies scream out in dismay, and what I see frightens me just the same.
Brown unleashes Bubba, as she takes flight off of all fours in my direction, with light from the mobs flames reflectin'off of her nigga-nibblers. I raise my hand to the airborne beast demanding complete obedience. As I recite my protection chant Bubba's body locks up, jaws foam and she hit's the ground as if she ran into a brick wall. She looks up at me and runs off cowerin' and whimperin' leavin' her

master and the mob in her dust. They had seen Bubba do a lot of things, but never run from someone she was to attack.

"May!! What you done did to my Bubba? They sed you's a witch!!"

"No witch sheriff… Saint. Now I told you I'd bring em' out."

So for a second time, I turn to go into the house to have my kinfolks face justice, but I guess my nephews decided they had a train to catch and wanted nothing to do with turning themselves in. I hear gunfire coming from the back of the house and see my kinfolk running across the yard tryin' to get better shots at the bloodthirsty white men. I gather all my babies and we all lay flat on the floor and I told them not to get up. I prayed like I never prayed before, asking the Lord to guide those bullets and let them fall where they may, just not near none of mine. The gunfight only lasted a couple of minutes but it seems like an eternity when you have eight lives needn' to be accounted for. When the smoke cleared the mob was short six men. I had two wounded nephews and four others that had gotten away. I have a feeling I won't be seeing them anymore, especially if they were able to make that train. But most importantly me and my babies are sound. Sheriff Brown gathered up the two injured Thomas boys and the rest of the mob collected the dead. Brown vowed that his two nigger captures were injured men now but would be dead men by morning. And then I knew what was coming next.

"Alright May hand over yo' boy. I ain't gone kill' em, and I'll do my best to make sure these men do the same, but mark my words when I say this boy won't see not one day of freedom as long as I have breath in my body!!"

As I look in my baby eyes they begin overflowing with tears from fear. I remind him trouble don't last always and Brown couldn't keep him forever. I told him to pray day and night and informed him I would come see him every morning as long as I had breath in my body. I couldn't believe I was walking my oldest child out to hand him over to a group of men who wanted to see him dead, but here I am doing just that. But before I do, I need to remind Brown of my expectations.

"Brown, you killin' those two men thas between you and the Lord, you have to answer for that and I can't vouch for them cuz I ain't they mammy… but mine? Do not lay a finger on my baby sheriff; I'm expecting you to honor my wishes."

Brown gestures for one of his deputies to secure Cecil as my baby cries out, "I love you mama!"

And I answer as I had done for years to all my children,
"Always, baby always."

Brown heads out my gate but turns with a message for my relatives.

"May, you tell them no good nigger nephews of yours they better hope they make it to Chicago, and if they do they better not ever step foot nowhere in the south ever again or they will be shot on sight. C'mon !!"

And with that they were gone. Even though I have seven chillins still with me it doesn't lessen the hurt of loosin' one. I can only pray that Brown keeps his promise. This was the first time I'd let one of my babies down. I felt less of a mother...worthless at best. I couldn't even protect him, my own flesh and blood. But deep down I had this strange feeling this wouldn't be my last time sippin' from this cup.

3 MAH MAY

This morning came swift as if I had just blinked. I got no rest and if I did, no one told me. I woke with my mind stuck on Cecil and what I coulda done to avoid all this mess. I always vowed I wouldn't raise no heathens, liars or criminals, so no one would be able to say May's doing an injustice to the town with her bad seeds. I'd sooner be dead than to have that kinda talk going on 'bout me. I remember that my grannybabe always instilled in my uncles what she thought a man should be. I never knew my grandfather and no one ever spoke about him. I asked my mother about him once as a child but got a look that warned me that subject is off limits. Mother never cared to explain or elaborate, even as I became an adult, so I just embraced the fact that I came from powerful, strong women. Nothing more; nothing less. Never even brought it up again. I once heard my oldest uncle telling his brothers that they mama killed they daddy by praying him to death, but as a child, I thought it was a joke. Now it's my turn and I'm thinking, ain't nothing funny. As I try to reflect, Delilah continues talkin' my ears off as she's done on the whole walk to work and for the past two hours since we've been here. My Delilah was the oldest of my girls and she was working at the Governor's mansion just as I had at her age.

The difference between Delilah and myself is that my daughter has goals and ideas and none of her dreams entailed her working in no one's kitchen. And boy can this child talk, I'm trying to look interested but I think she can tell I was thinking 'bout last night while she's steady looking towards the future.

"Mama I don't wanna be no criminal like you nephews, trickin' people out they money, always lookin over yo shoulder, runnin' from state to state never putting down roots. I wanna be somebody, do sumthin wit my life. I want to go to college, read Langston Hughes and Claude McKay. Mama is you even listenin to me?"

I wasn't listening, still worried about my Cecil, but my baby girl needs me now too.
"I'm sorry baby, mama listenin'… you is somebody, you's one of God's creations *and* you's a Thomas. Besides, you know I can't afford to send you off to no college I can barely feed y'all as is."

"Sarah's going to college and I get much better marks than her."

Delilah tries to remind me in a tone that didn't fancy to well with me.

"Yeah you just might be right, but Sarah's white, rich, and the governor's granddaughter, three thangs which you ain't and sometimes in life it's not what you learn but who's giving the lessons."

"Thas not fair!" my baby pouts folding her arms. "I does my lessons, I studies and works hard at learnin', educatin' should be for everyone not just for the rich!"

"Well baby thas life in the south. Thas how it's been and how it's gone be til someone changes thangs. But never stop chasin' what you want you bound to catch it."

"They's got coloreds goin' to college in N'orleans." Delilah blurts out seeming to never be at a loss for words.

"Yeah and das dem creoled colored folk too. Dey have dey own towns, and dey own schools. You might look Creole chile but French you ain't."
I laugh cause sometimes my baby look mo' whiter than whites themselves and she still not ready to give up her fight.

"You sho bout dat?"
Delilah challenges as she begin stumbling through some basic French taught to her by one of my dearest friends Madame Bordeaux. We laugh and

hug almost not noticing Governor Gifton entering through the kitchen door.

"Mornin' Governor."
The rest of the staff and I chime out in unison as we had done every morning for the past forever.

"You ladies seem mighty jovial this morning considering last night's events." Gifton comments, looking at me over the top of his glasses.

"I spoke with the sheriff and he gave me his word he wasn't gone harm lil' Cecil at all. You might wanna take Brown a plate of food when you take your son his meal this evening."

"Will do sir and thank yo-"
As I try to show my appreciation, he ignores me and makes his way over to Delilah with a look in his eye that was very disturbing to me.

"Mornin Miss Delilah Ann, my you sholl done grow'd into quite the young lady."
He compliments eyein' my baby from head to toe.

"Mornin Gov'na Gifton."
Delilah sheepishly answers not taking her eyes off the lemons she was cutting for the afternoon lemonade.

"We were just laughin' wit Delilah as she shared one of her foolish notions about going to college and educatin' herself." I interrupt trying to divert the pervert's attention back to me and away from my baby.

"I told her when you's colored, the only colors needed for education is white and green, two colors we know nuthin bout." I joked trying to lighten the mood but Gifton found nothing funny.

"On the contrary May, look at this gal, smart, attractive and sounds like she's very ambitious."

As the governor rambles on I notice Delilah now looking at him, and the defeat that was in her eyes a few minutes ago has now turned back to hope.

"I think this child deserves to further her learnin' when the time comes, what you say Delilah? Let me get a good look at you gal."
Gifton grabs Delilah's hand and spins her as if they were doing a waltz and with that, I think I've had enough.

"Governor please don't go filling her head with all that nonsense. She'll be just fine working alongside us colored's right here in the kitchen sir."
I catch myself as I almost raise my voice hating I even brought the subject up.

"Well I'm sorry May and as governor of the great state of Louisiana, I say she's too pretty to work in anybody's kitchen, not even the finest of kitchens such as mine. So I think we may need to start looking for a college to send this young lady to."

"SIR?!" Delilah and I exclaim in disbelief.

"Why of course after your last promotion of course, but you will need to start preparing early. Can an old man get a hug?"

The fat pudgy man extends his arms and Delilah so overcome with joy runs right into them. I snatch Delilah up by the collar and fling her back to her lemons in one motion. She looked as if she was about to voice her objections but when she saw the look in my eyes she knew this was not the time.

"Thanks, but no thanks governor, we's proud folk. If I wanted to send her to college I will work in ten white folk kitchens but until then we's fine."
I stress my point hoping that would be the end of it.

"Well, sorry to inform you May, you work for me and I will always have the final say. Now this child is going to college, you'll see her on holidays and summer breaks. I'll pay for tuition, room and board. I will personally make sure she has a wardrobe fit for college life. She'll be like dem dere umm, creoles, look jes like em too! Where you get dat light skin and pretty hair from, you sholl ain't got it from ya mammy cuz she black as tar and ugly to boot?"

"Daddy I s'ppose?" Delilah answers not caring to spare my feelings.

"C'mon Delilah lets go and talk about this in more detail."

"But I must finish slicing the lemons sir."

"Ya mama can do it. May, I'm going to go speak with Delilah a spell so bring the pitcher with two glasses into the parlor when you finish the ade."

"Will do governor."

I politely answer when I really want to break the arm he done placed in the small of my baby's back leading her out the room and down the hall. I done laughed off gossip about the horrific things the good ol'governor does with young girls, but I never thought, after all I done heard from settlement to settlement, that he would get his paws on mine. The kitchen staff were all staring at me for a reaction but quickly went back to work once I gave dem tha 'mind ya business glare'. I shake my head because I don't like where this is headed not one bit.

4 MAH MAY

Time and years fly by, and the struggles that I've
endured seemed to have nested on my face. As I
look at my reflection and see how I've aged, it's
no secret that it hasn't been graceful. It's as if my
appearance is trying to tell the world my story,
yelling every secret and prayer locked deep in my
heart. My skin shouted my story by way of wrinkle
patterns congregating and dispersing where they
may. A maze of sorts leading to my heart strings.
Every emotion conjured up inside of me played out
in a wrinkle on my face. I had been so familiar
with these tell-tale scars that I could just about
recount how I got each and every one of my
creases. My mahogany skin is starting to look
more like thick, worn, cheap leather thanks to a
combination of field work, hot southern summers
and a lifetime of seeing things that would drive a
sane man crazy. As I literally watched another
wrinkle forming, I thought about Cecil and the
determination and endurance he has shown
through the years. And it seemed the newly
discovered wrinkle was quickly establishing itself
the harder I thought about Cecil's situation. At that
moment it dawned on me that I have never missed
a day to visit, even when I was thought to have
pneumonia, which turned out to be a terrible cold,
either way, nothing was gonna stop me from
seeing my baby boy. But even though years passed

and things changed, the sheriff was man enough to keep his word and never sent my baby off to one of those state chain gangs or allowed the drunken lynch mobs to hang my boy. Sheriff Brown soon found Cecil to be quite the handy man. So all the odd jobs around the jail and Browns own personal home were all worked by Cecil. Besides, I think another reason he kept Cecil around was because he liked the meals I would bring to them every evening. I knew this to be the case once Brown started making special dinner request or taking it upon himself to make up a menu of sorts. Certain days of the week he wanted certain meals. I only agreed to it once Cecil said It was okay. This was my son's dinner, not his jailer. But just as God spoiled me from birth, he allowed my son to love his keeper and I'm sure deep down Brown loved him too. That's what I tried to teach my children to always try and find 'your' silver lining. Try and make the best of a horrible situation because what doesn't kill us will enhance. I had raised all my children by myself and never thought to marry again even when people was telling me that my chaps needed a daddy around. Men came a callin' but I had no interest in any of them. They didn't want me; I reckon the one-hundred and sixty acres was more attractive than an old woman with eight babies. But I never paid any of that no mind. My grannybabe raised to me to be independent and be grateful for a companion but not dependent on him. As I brush my matted salt and pepper locks and roll it into a bun, pinning it in the top of my head, I think about my children, their father and our first meeting. I knew marrying that hi-yella Chicagoan would come back on me someday, but I never thought it would manifest through my brood. It's as if the complexion of my children will determine their quality of life. My lighter complect'd seeds path seems to be lined with more opportunities that aren't there for my darker offspring. But with that brings other worries for the lighter ones. Through my years I have come to learn certain things, one of those being that colored men seem to be more attracted to lighter skinned women than the darker toned ones. But what I was learning first hand from my Delilah was that not only is it Negroes that like the hi-yella heifers, but the white men too, and Gov. Gifton would be no exception. The good ol' governor kept his word sending my baby off to college for the next two years taking care of every expense just as he said, but I know one day he will be expecting a pay out on his investment. One day, pay day gone have to come.

"Quittin' time ladies. Y'all hurry and finish up so I can get this food over to the jail for Cecil and Brown."

I instructed my workers as I finished up making plates for the two men but was interrupted by a knock at the door.

"Mama!!" Delilah screams as she greets me with a hug and a kiss before I knew what was even happening.

"Chile, its break already?"

"Yeah mah! You don't seem too pleased, aren't you happy to see me?"

"Of course mama happy to see you, it's just I almost didn't even recognize my baby, look at you all grown up and sophisticated like. You remind me of one of them socialites I be seeing in Mrs. Gifton magazines. Give me a twirl baby."
Delilah puts down her leather pocketbook and a copy of Richard Wrights Native Son as she twirls and spins til we laugh, cry and then embrace.

"You really surprised me Delilah, I guess I been so busy worryin' about you that I paid no mind to break being here. And it look like you been worried about sumthin too, who'd a thought you could get any smaller than you already were? Here chile eat this, I'll make ya brother another plate."
I hand my rail-of-a-child the plate and she went to work on it.

"So sit down and tell mama what the good ol' governors money done taught you this term." I ask my baby noticing how proper she was talkin' now. All her 'dey' and 'dems' had turned into 'they' and 'them'. She sounded more confident and sure of herself. Then I noticed a ring on her finger and it's almost like she's trying to hide it, but she ought to know by now she can't get nothing past her mama. Lord, is my child married? Anyone would want her, she beautiful and smart. Lord, Lord. Please help me this day.

"Mah I've learned so much this past year. Last year I was so caught up in focusing on other people, trying to fit in, even to the point of acting like them, I wasn't being myself. But this year, oh mama, this year my eyes have been opened. I listen to Count Basie, I've been exposed to so many different writers even went to hear Marion Anderson sing at the Washington Monument in D.C."
Delilah rambled on and on nonstop. She seemed to have a story for every topic that came up. You could hear the excitement oozing out her voice. I want to cry tears of joy seeing my baby so happy but it sounds like our good time is about to take a turn.

"Mama you would never guess what they got going on for coloreds out in the world. There's groups out there whose only mission is to get equal rights for colored folk. Soon there will be no more segregation no more white-only this or colored-only that."

Delilah was so animated and enthusiastic in her speech until she had her feelings hurt by the burst of laughter from the kitchen staff, including myself.

"Chile what you talkn' we lives in the south, this is how it's been and how it's gone continue to be."
I inform Miss Lady as I make another plate of food for Cecil.

"They are called the N.A.A.C.P. They been marching the streets of New York since 1917. They do great things for coloreds, soon we will be able to learn, work and live with white folk, even vote, women too!!"

By this time, all us in the kitchen are holding our stomachs from laughing so hard. The more we laughed the more frustrated Delilah became.

"I'm glad you all think this is so hilarious, but I didn't think it was that funny when I was voted president of our college chapter."

The laughter stopped immediately, partly due to the announcement by the young blactivist. But the main reason was because Gifton had been standing there the whole time watching Delilah proclaim her new found ethnicity. The look that was coming from his face wasn't one of approval, it was clear he didn't like what he was seeing or hearing.

"Wait. What was that Miss Delilah?" Gifton asks glaring at Delilah over the top of his glasses.

"Afternoon governor and I believe you heard me correctly. But in case you didn't, I said that I am the president of a club at my school that fights for the civil rights of coloreds. So one day we can vote and make decent wages and people like my mama ain't gotta work for white folk like you... you all can do it yourself."
Delilah informs the governor matter-of-factly, with hand on hip, finger and neck justa swaying.

"Is that right young lady? Well in case you didn't know, niggas ain't civil so they don't need no rights and I ain't payin' for you to be joinin' no clubs and getting' yo head filled with all dat nonsense. I thought you was different, but you jes like the rest, maybe even worse, at least other niggas know how to stay in a niggas place!"

"Hold on now governor…don't take that tone with my child. Thas why I didn't want you doin nuthin fo us that we hadn't earned. Now I'll deal with her when I get home!"

I knew three years ago this day was gone come, and I'm still not ready for it.

"Oh no need mama, I can handle the good ol' governor. And don't worry I done earned every no-good, low-down penny he ever spent on me. Yeah the good ol' governor ain't too civil himself…he like to touch little girls, make them do favors what he call it."

Before I know it I done jumped up and slapped tha shit out of Delilah for talking like that bout Gifton.

"Delilah Ann Thomas!! You watch yo mouth, I will not have you saying such thangs bout him!"

"No mah, it's true…true as true can be. Been doing it for years, I was shame to tell you because I wanted to go to school so bad I just never said nothing. But no more…I ain't scared and I ain't lying!"

"You little bitch!! All the money I done spent on you and this is how you repay me?"

"Is this true Gifton?" I asks as I spot the butcher knife out the corner of my eye where I had been slicing the ham, now I'm thinking about slicing a turkey.

"All truth in it mah, he's a filthy, dirty…"

Before my baby finished her statement the governor slaps Delilah to the floor but just as quick me and my knife was on him. The kitchen ladies who were acting like they weren't paying attention all ran over to me scared of what my next move would be.

"DO! NOT! HIT! MY! CHILD! AGAIN! Do you understand? I told you I will deal with her when I gets home!"

"You niggers get out of my house! Don't ever step foot on my property again. May I trusted you for thirty-five years, you helped raise my children and they's children. You fuckin' nigger bitch!!"

"And I never hit not a one of them, and you won't be hitting on mine!!"

I gladly pack my belongings as Delilah gathers her things with a look of pride and accomplishment all over her face.

"Thas why niggas don't need no educatin' they start to thank they too good, but guess what, you still jes a nigga always will be a nigga!!"

Gifton went on and on, the madder he got the more we laughed. As we left the mansion which I knew would be for the last time we walked hand in hand holding our heads high leaving the governor red as a beet and the kitchen ladies snickering under they breaths. We walked the distance to the jail in silence. I guess we both were thinking over the afternoons events. We visited with Cecil and talked about the family, we didn't feel the need to tell him about Gifton the boy had enough to worry 'bout as is.

5 DELILAH

"I'm glad you didn't mention to Cecil what happened with Gifton."
I inform Delilah as we continue our journey home together.

"Cecil would have killed him for sure, mama, I'm truly sorry about your job, I know it meant a lot to you."
Delilah apologizes trying to be sincere as possible, but I could tell she was elated she was able to expose the governor and take away his power.

"Jehovah Jireh."

"What did you say mama?"

"Jehovah Jireh….baby, Lord our Provider, he been allowin' me to take care of y'all all these years he ain't gone stop now." I advise my baby. Her with all her college educating still having so much to learn about life.

"That was really grown up of you to apologize like dat, but it wasn't yo fault, Gifton the one who got a problem…not you. And I would like to apologize about yo' schoolin', you seemed to light up whenever you spoke about it, I know you loved it, we just gone have to tighten up to try and see if we can send you off to a college ourselves someday."

"That's just it mama, you ain't gone have to worry 'bout me no more, that's what I came to the governor's mansion to talk to you about."

I stop and look at my Delilah and I think I might know what she bout to say.

"Mama I met a man! And not just any man, he's special. I've never met anyone like him before. He's in the military, educated, and well-traveled and, well…we're getting married!"
Delilah throws up her hand displaying the ring I caught a glimpse of at the governor's mansion.

"What you talkin' bout child? How you just gone up and marry some stranger?"

"That's just it mah, he's not a stranger. I've known him for close to a year now, I met him in the last term of my first year in school. His name is Bobby Nelson, and he left school before graduating to enlist in the army. He's getting stationed out in California and asked me to come with him. Mama, I'm marrying this man, I love him."

"So not only are you tellin' me you gettin' married, but that you movin' to California too?"

It was like someone pulled the rug from under my feet, this had to be a joke. My baby finally home and now she's leaving me? It might as well be for good since California seems like a life time away.

"I want you to come with us, you and my brothers and sisters. Bobby will be living at the army base, only coming home on weekends and I'll be in that big ol' house all by myself. See mama, we can finally be free, free to be colored and nothing be wrong with it. Oh can't you see it mama!"

"I know you must be in love with him, he got yo head all up in the clouds. Y'all dumb-in-love if you thank me and seven children could just jump up and move clear across the world. Thas crazy talk!"

"It's not crazy talk mama, that's what white folks want you to think that we can't make it if we leave the south, it's a whole new world out there for us, we gotta go find it. You always told me to never stop chasing what I want, I'm bound to catch it, well I wants freedom, I wants to be free and not have to worry 'bout no Giftons or Sheriff Browns…"
Delilah stops mid-sentence as if she saw a ghost. Delilah was so caught up in herself she forgot about Cecil, and she knew I wouldn't leave Louisiana with him in Brown's jail.

"Baby, you've always been my dreamer. You always wanted something better out of life. But yo dreams can't be my dreams. If yo happiness is in California with that man, then go. I always want my baby to be happy. But for me, right now, mama's happiness is here in my home, with my family, health and strength. But by all means, I want you to go, ain't like mama can't come visit."
I grab my baby and give her the biggest hug a proud mother could give before we continue on home. I trust Delilah and I know she will be marrying a nice, hardworking, respectable gentleman…but I still needed to see if he was bona fide.

"So who's this man who done swept my baby off her feet?"

"Mama I told you his name is Bobby, a wonderful man, but you will get to see for yourself tonight at dinner"

"Dinner…Tonight?"
I stop and look at my daughter like she done lost her cotton picking mind.

"Yes tonight mah I invited him to dinner, I hope you're not mad."

I continue walking at a quicker pace than before.

"Mama what's wrong? You okay? Why you walking so fast?"

"Well, I guess I needs to get home and get dinner on for my new son-in-law don't ya think?"

"Oh mama, you're the greatest...Love you!" Delilah squeals as she runs to catch up with my almost trot.

And I answer like any other time.
"Always, baby always. What a day....what a day."

We continue down the path past the barns and run down make shift houses; the change of scenery was letting us know we were nearing home. We laugh about Gifton some more when Delilah gets a disturbing look on her face, and tries for me not to notice. I look to see what or who has Delilah so stuck, when I see my daughter Mabeleen coming out the bushes with who looks to be Mr. Henry from up the road. Delilah runs up ahead of me to confront her sister.

"Mabeleen Maybell Thomas, what you doing out here actin like a jezebel?"

Delilah jumps in Mabel 's face and pushes poor Mr. Henry, who through all the commotion loses his pants and run's off with his trousers around his ankles.

"Well, well, well big sis, you finally done came to see how the poor folk live huh?"
Mabeleen snaps as she notices the new and improved Delilah.

Delilah grabs Mabel by the wrist just as I catch up to where the girls are.

"Don't be grabbin' on me! Who do you think you are?"

"I'm your ….is that alcohol Mabel? You're drunk!"

"Mabel, whas goin' on here?"
I find myself asking a question I already knew the answer to.

"Mind yo own business old woman!" Mabel yells.

"You watch your mouth; don't be talking to mama like that!"

"Like what? You're never here to talk to her at all, so what you talkin? Look everyone, Miss Smarty pants came to see us po' folk, Miss Education, Miss I'm so pretty cuz I'm damn near white…"

Delilah shoves her little sister trying to make her take back the comments she just made.

"You watch what you say; I done worked hard for all my learning!"

"You mean, you done worked the governor hard…"

And that's all it took for the two ladies to commence to fighting right there in the dirt road. I watch the screaming and hair pulling for a few seconds, then continued on my journey, humming a hymnal and shaking my head.

Mabeleen, the overly developed child of mine. Gal looked like a grown woman at the age of 12. Had breast and hips some older women never acquire in a lifetime. I had been chasing men and boys away from her since she was a child. Even though she was smart, the attention from the opposite sex took any vigor she had about learning and being taught anything. Girl head is hard as a rock and only seemed to be open to shenanigans and no good. Always in some trouble and would disappear for days on-in when her no-good Chicago cousins came down to visit. Lord knows I tried my best with Mable and I know I must take all blame for anything she may be other than a child of God as my grannybabe use to say, " *I aint never seen bad children, only bad parents.* " Even with all my efforts Mable was the promiscuous of all my girls once she realized that she could get a man to do just about anything she wanted them to. Mable wasn't bad, just not too mindful of my or others feelings. As long as Mableen was happy, it didn't matter how others were left feeling. Through the years Mable went from liking boys to men at an age when she should have been playing with dolls. But none of that didn't matter to her. I tried beating her, threatening her and even locking her up one time, nothing stopped my child. Once I put it in the Lord's hands, I was never hard on Mabel again, even felt bad for her at times. Out of all the men she be 'entertaining' she never had a man of her own, always borrowed some other woman's man. She already had two children and she was currently pregnant by who some say is one of my nephews who got away in the shoot out some years ago. He had been sneaking in and out of town, making a liar out of Brown all this time. Whether Mabel was pregnant or not, you wouldn't be able to tell by her figure. Mabel had wide, welcoming, child bearing hips, so a baby had all the room in the world to hide. She wasn't fair skinned at all; she took after my side of the family in the complexion area. She always said she would only have children by light to fair skinned men so her children wouldn't have to go thru life being so black. Mabel wasn't as pretty as Delilah or as smart, but had no problem catching a man, the problem comes in when it's time to keep the men. She can't seem to lock em' down. And that just fine with Mabel since she liked to drink and go to Big Sook's juke joint any night of the week…and she would be there, with child or not.

6 Delilah

"Mabel we can't keep fighting forever!"

We look at each other and laugh at how ridiculous we must seem to on seekers.

"Mabel you my little sister and I don't want you to be out here giving yourself away to just anybody. Like some common whore. You special, you should act as such."

I advise, as I look down at the rips and tears in some of the best clothes I own.

"That's easy for you to say though Delilah, you've always had it good, always. Light is right, could do no wrong. You had life on a platter served up to you on the daily. Why couldn't I ever go to school, or go get a decent job or even a decent man? When mama sent us to clean for whites in town, I always had to do field or yard work while you watched and sometimes even played with their children. So I have to use the only thang that works for me, my body and sex. That's all I got. That's how I get my attention and believe me sis, growing up behind you, bad attention is better than no attention at all."

Mabel burst out crying, I guess she must have wanted to tell me this for so long. I stand and offer my baby sis a hand getting up. To which she reciprocates; I then dust off her skirt as she wipes the tears from her eyes.

"Well lil sis, I thinks you're beautiful, you've always taken up for me whenever the colored kids said I wasn't black enough or the white kids accused me of trying to be like them. I didn't pick my skin color, it picked me. You don't know what I've went through at college and even here in town. It's been no bed of roses, mama just taught me how to suck certain things up and chose my battles wisely. I guess we've been dealing with some of the same issues separately, but I do thank God for the times you were able to be there for me. I guess we all hurt, just in different ways. Besides nobody wanted to fight you, not only did you like the boys, you fought like them too!"

We laugh and hug, happy that things were better between us than it had been in a long time. Mable lays her head on my shoulder then looks at me with a sincere yet devious smirk.

"I guess I'mma have to go back to fightn' for my men while your home for the summer huh?"

"Not this time sis. I's getting married. Moving to California!"

I proudly show her my ring and even more proudly tell her *all* about Bobby, you know that stuff I couldn't share with mama, and Mable took it all in. Even giving me some tips and tricks she said I'm gone need in the bedroom. I was shame, but was all ears. My sister and I talked while we walked hand in hand all the way home. We haven't done this since we were children. Love her.

~~~~~

"Okay everyone, here he come and *please* don't nobody shame me."

I instruct the whole Thomas clan as I line the boys up to look like little angels, if that was possible. Mabeleen and Daisy Mae, my youngest sister, run over to the window to see my new beau come up the road.

"They's two of them, who dat with him?" Daisy asks with a twisted face.

I had an idea who it was, but I had to look to be sure.

"Oh that's Joseph Freeman, he's Bobby best friend from the Army…that's my Bobby there on the right, the cute one."

"*Ooowee*, well that must be my Joseph on the left. I jes loves a man in uniform." Mabel blurts out running to go fix her hair.

"I don't think they's nothing to look at me myself."
Daisy confesses as she watches Mabel get all gussied up for a man she don't even know.

"Daisy you don't know nuthin bout a man, let alone a Army man, let yo big sister show you how it's done." Mabel responds as she sashays past us fixing her breast to make them perkier than they really are as she heads out on the porch to greet the men.

"Don't pay her no mind Daisy Mae, you know she boy crazy. You will find you a man soon enough, besides, you too young to be thinking about men right now anyway. You wanna end up like her all kids no man?"
Daisy laughs and gives me a hug and we join Mabel outside as the men head up the path to our porch.

"Hey!!! There's my baby!!"

Bobby yells as he grabs me and flings me around but not before planting a big wet one on my lips.

"Sisters, this here is Bobby. Bobby these my sisters."

"Hey." The ladies sang in unison.

"Ladies." Bobby greets the ladies with a kiss on their hands then turns to bring the strange man into view.

"Ladies, this here is my good friend Joe. He's studying to be a pilot over in Tuskegee."

He greets the ladies in the same manner as Bobby had. "Evening Ladies."

"Hey." The ladies answer together again as if on cue.

"And by the way, my name is Joseph. I'm learning to be an 'airman'. That's what they call us Bobby not pilots, they say we the first of its kind, you know being colored airmen and all."
Joseph corrects Bobby topping it off with a roll of his eyes.

Mah May must have been listening from inside the house because she waited til there was a pause in conversation to ask us if we were eating out on the porch, so naturally we all took it as a clue to come inside. And when mama drops her hints, you better take heed real fast.

"Let me see who gone be marrying my daughter."

Mah announces as she walks over to greet the men. Even though she had never met Bobby, once she saw him she knew instantly that he was her new son-in-law. Mama just had this thing about her, like an extra sense.

"Welcome to my home and to my family Bobby. We ain't got a lot, but what we do have you's welcomed to it."

Mah extends her greeting hand but Bobby chose to disregard that and gives Mah a hug so big it lifted her off the ground.

"Thanks Mah May, but how'd you know I was Bobby?"

"It's not so much I knew you…I knows my child. And she been talking 'bout getting married since she was toddlin', she been fantasizin' bout her perfect man as long as I could remember and you tha spittin' image of all that she dreamt about."

We all laugh at mama's rationale as I watch Bobby make his way over to my little brothers that were still lined up as I had left them, but starting to get antsy.

Booby walks the line of youngster a couple of times before he spoke one word.

"Well, I think I've heard enough about these young men to be able and call 'em by name" Bobby looks at the first in line and bends his six-foot-three inch frame eye level with the nervous boy.

"This little fellow here is Nathaniel, huh? Boy I heard you be knocking fools out like Joe Lewis…am I right?"

"I's can fight; but I ain't little, I'm gone be in the army too! Hey, how you know my name anyways?" Nathaniel asks Bobby looking puzzled. Bobby laughs with his eyes fixed on the next in line.

"Well I'm gone be your brother, I'm supposed to know you aint I? And not only you, I know all y'all's name. Why, this here is Augustus, he and J.C's fourteen year old twins. Augustus is the sanger of the family, boy I heard you sang like nobody's business be having half the church shouting down the aisles. And J.C, you're the family craftsman, hands blessed by God."

Bobby leaves the two young boys blushing with his compliments also wondering if he had mind reading powers as he makes his last introduction.

"And this here be the baby of the clan, the athlete, Thomas Thomas, but they's call you Tommy. Heard you so quick you can out run jackrabbits boy!"

"Yes sir, sometimes." Tommy humbly admits.

Bobby had gone down the line getting every name and attribute correct of all the brothers. I watch him as he continues speaking with the boys as mama gets my attention from across the room and gives me a slight wink as her own personal stamp of approval.

"Where's Mr. Thomas?"

Joseph innocently asks getting no answer only a very threatening look from Bobby.

"Let's eat."
Mah May announces ignoring the question.

MABEL

At dinner my brothers were all smitten with
Bobby, hell, even Mah May and she ain't neva
took a likin to any of the men that came callin on
her girls. The whole family was laughin at the
stories he and Joseph were telln about the army
while Delilah staring lost in his eyes. She looks so
determined to be a good wife and I could tell she
was willing to follow this man to the ends of the
Earth. She always won; she always came out on
top, every time. When all I ever had was buzzards
luck. But no more, it's time for me to win, starting
now.

"I's clear the table mama."

Daisy volunteers as I glance over at Joseph as he
finishes his sweet bread.

"Ummm Joseph, you wanna join me out on the
porch while we finish our lemonade?"

I ask so seductively that no man could say no. As I
begin to excuse myself from the table headin'
towards the front door, I couldn't believe what I
was hearin'…

"Sorry Miss Mabeleen, I thinks I'll help Miss
Daisy with the dishes…if that's alright with you
Miss Daisy?"
Joseph answered looking uncomfortable waiting
for my little sister to give him the okay.

"Sho. Fine by me!"
She finally answered leaving Joseph excited but
me looking stupid. How he gone pick an
inexperienced child over me? With all this I'm
packing.

"Well fine then! I'mma go to Big Sook's!"
I stomp out the house as my family seems to be
tickled by my getting angry. But I don't pay 'em
no mind. Big Sook's my playground; I can have
any and as many men I want on any given night.
So with my sweater and a cigarette in hand along
with a song in my heart, I hum my way out to the
gate.

"Mabel…Mabeleen."

"Who dat?"

"Wait up it's me Gus."

"Boy what you doin' out here Mah May gone skin you alive."
I warn and continue on my way.

"Wait. Tell Big Sook I's be there once mama go to sleep."

"Mah gone get you. Keep sneakin' off to Sook's sangin that devil music if you want to."

"But he pays me good money."

I finally stop to listen to hear what Gus has to say as he pulls out close to fifty dollars that had been crumbled up in his pocket.

"Does Mah May know you got all dat money?"

"No! And she ain't gotta know either."

"Well it looks like I'm gonna need some quiet money. I'll say, ten dollars now and five dollars every time you sang, and this could be our little secret."
I advise Gus as I count out my issue before he is even able to agree.

"Fine….just tell Sook I'll be there."

"Oh yeah, tonight I want you to sang that song I like… what's the one you wrote about the loose woman that all the men in town wanted?"

"You mean Kissin' Clara?"

"*GUS!*"
We hear Mah May call from inside the house.

"Comin' Mah!"
Gus responds looking spooked hoping I keep his secret as he runs back to the house.

"Yeah, I'll tell Sook you be there, if Mah don't kill you first. I think to myself as I hide my hush money in my bosom and continue on down the road sangin' Kissin' Clara."

7 DAISY

"That was a mighty fine dinner Mah May."
Bobby compliments as we all sit out on the porch
finishing up our lemonade. Mah had made the
younger children stay inside and get ready for bed.
Normally this would have included Daisy, but Mah
let her join in since Joseph seemed to be taking a
liking to her.

"Sholl hope my baby can cook like her mama."

Bobby jokes as he wraps his arms around me from
behind, embarrassing me in front of my mother.

"Honey chile, ain't too much Delilah can't do. She
was my right hand when it came to raisin these
chillins. She learned how to cook, clean and care
for her siblings as I was popping them out."

"We gone have us a whole bunch of kids too!"
Bobby laughs rubbing my stomach like I was with
child.

"Him just playing mama."
I jump in, putting a halt to Bobby and his big
mouth.

"He ain't playin' child. Yo daddy and I had ten chillins, the Lord saw fit that only eight survived. Oh Delilah, yo father would have been so proud of you two, he woulda tried to scare the dickens out of poor Bobby here with one of the most sternest speeches he could conjure up about bein' a man and takin' care of his baby. But he woulda been mighty proud…God Rest his Soul."
Mah shuffles back into the house humming a hymn and shaking her head leaving us out on the porch by ourselves.

"Miss Daisy, if you don't mind, may I ask you a question?"
Joseph looks like it took all the courage in the world just to ask permission to ask the question.

"Sho Joseph, whas on yo mind?"

"Well, if you don't mind me asking…What happened to your father? I'm mean, I know he's passed, but how'd it happened? No disrespect of course."

Bobby jumps in his friend's face, "Nun ya man! None you damn business."
Still not backing down but standing toe to toe with his boy ready to knock Joseph on his ass.

"Calm down Brother Bobby."

Daisy responds, "It's okay, he really wanna know, I's tell em… What happened to my daddy *humm*, how can I put this? Well, some say mama kilt him."

"Your own mama?"
The two men sound off in unison, Bobby defenses now down.

"Yesss, Mah May. Das what folk say."
Daisy informs the men even more carefree than before.

"Thas right, prayed him to death."
I jump in taking over where Daisy had left off.

"My mama is a descendant of a very proud tribe of spiritual worshipers from Africa. When the white men came and tried to capture them back in their homeland, there were stories of men and women disappearing and levitating before the white men's eyes. The evil intruders were so spooked by the never seen powers they had to pay other tribe members to trick and capture this unique group of people. This was all from the powers and the faith they had in their prayers. Some say they were a special tribe, a chosen people, only a few of them were ever caught with my great-grandmother being one of them. When my mama was a child, my grannybabe taught her their way of life, she also taught mama that just because you have the power, you don't abuse it, you need to know how and when to use this gift. She taught her when to pray, how to pray and what to pray for. And so since mama had all this runnin' thru her veins, as she got older, she decided to help others in need of blessings or miracles. So all the local folk come to mama when they are in need of prayer: cheating man, the women come to mama; bad harvest or crop, they come to mama. She is considered a Saint by the coloreds and a witch by white folks."

I continue to school the men since they were so curious about my daddy. But by now their mouths were hanging wide open and I don't even think they realized it themselves. I keep on with my story, not paying the men no mind.

"Tale has it that daddy had another family up in Chicago and would leave home for a spell not coming back for months on in. He would only come back long enough to father a child, and all the while taking care of another woman even making babies with her. And not just one woman, a woman up the road, the next county over, the next parish over, so on and so forth. At times he would be living within eye-shot of mama, just a rearing his other family right where mama could see him, leaving her to have to fend for herself with all these kids. There were even men who my daddy gave permission to come call on mama, but she would never come out the room to meet them. Around that time she rarely got out of the bed let alone got out the house. She was suffering from a broken heart, it was paining her so. Then I guess one morning it came too much for mama to bear. It was wrecking her soul so much til she just fell to her knees and started praying. And not just any ol' kind of prayer, but one from the deep down in her hurt. And not like we are talking to where you could understand, but in her native tongue, which she rarely uses. It's told there's only a few left who can even speak or understand it. She prayed all that morning, thru the noon day, and well into the night. Mama did that for three days straight, never once stopping to eat, go bathroom or take care of one child. I guess her ancestors heard her cry and pleaded to God on her behalf to have his way with daddy, and by the end of the third day of mama praying, daddy came walking up the path, ill as sin, and dropped dead soon as he stepped one foot in the door."

I grab and drink my lemonade while the two men look upon me in disbelief.

"Took six men to pry the dead body out of mama's arms when they came to bury him. She said daddy was finally home and wasn't nobody gone take him away from her." Daisy finished the story as she had started, very calm and matter-of-factly. By this time the hair was standing up on the back of the men's neck as they both stared at the threshold entrance into the house.

"Y'all'ss pulling our legs."
Joseph says trying to convince himself as such.

"Truth as truth could be, you said you wanted to know, well now you know." Daisy reminds Joseph.

"Enough with that Daisy Mae before ol' Bobby here thinks I'm gone pray him to death, no worries. I ain't a saint like mama. Mo' devil in me than good…an right now I thinks the devil in me wanna gone over to Big Sooks and have's me some fun before my baby leaves me again."

I dance over to Bobby to try and lighten the mood.

"You know mama ain't gone let me go. She gone say I's too young."
Daisy leans in and whispers to me, but the men overheard.

"I'mma ask her" Joseph stutters.

"What" we all whisper-yell.

"I'm going to ask Mah May could Daisy join us."

Joseph jumps up enjoying Daisy's company so much so that he was even willing to face Mah May and all her powers. He heads into the house but first hesitating as he crosses the threshold into the house.

Inside we hear talking, muffled voices then silence. Joseph came out with a bowed head and a look of defeat. Then he yells, "What y'all waiting for, let's go!"
Daisy yelled a big ol thank you Mah May as we all laugh and walk the winding road to the juke joint. I had been there times before, but tonight's crowd seems livelier than usual. The Army men were all enjoying one last night of fun before they were to report back to base. Other soldiers knew they would soon have duties of some sort in the war, so they were trying to have as much fun as possible. Booze was flowing and the music was blaring. The first person we recognized as we were getting closer to the entrance was Mabeleen, but she didn't stop to speak. She was entertaining two men who seem to have both taken a liking to her. Daisy and I both sipped shine from our date's jars enhancing the mood, while joining in on the festivities of the night. We all laugh and dance and didn't mind when our dates got in a feel or two on our hot, sweaty bodies. Towards closing time Sook got on stage and introduced his final act of the night.

"Ladies and gentlemen, I hope you all had fun tonight, but the nights not over, not by a long shot. Coming to the stage is an act I personally discovered myself, with no further ado, 'BABY GUS & THE GUSTINES!!"

I hadn't paid much attention to the stage since I was so caught up in Bobby, but once the music started and the lead singer got one note out his mouth, Daisy and I both jumped up and yelled, "AUGUSTUS!"
I knew it was him before I even laid eyes on him. I had been hearing that boy sing for the past thirteen years and he sounds better than ever.

"*Ooowee*! That boy knows he can sang!"
Joseph yells trying to mouth the words to 'Kissin Clara' a song he'd never even heard before.

"And look at them back round singers! With bodies like that, they got to be grown women."

Bobby adds as I give him the evil eye.

We dance and sing enjoying Gus' performance. He hadn't noticed us all night until he was halfway through his final song, then he really showed out. He was swaying and gyrating his hips even had women passing out. He tore up the stage giving it all he had, knowing his secret would be safe with us. We all left the juke joint singing 'Kissin Clara' just as the crowd was demanding an encore from the group.

"Now y'all have to promise y'all won't go tellin' Mah May bout my brothers new job."
Bobby comments partway home as we stop to admire the stars.

"As long as you promise you won't get yourself killed messin' around with dat 'ol Hitler."
I respond hating sometimes that Bobby was even in the military.

"Daisy, I had fun with you tonight, I don't want it to end."
Joseph purrs lost in Daisy's spell.

"I had fun too, but where else is there to go but home. It's late."

"Come with me." Joseph grabs Daisy's hand as they run off giggling making their way in the direction we had just come from.

"Bye!!"
I yell out finally happy Daisy found someone to call on her. I then look over at my Bobby as he kindly rubs the pain out my feet from all the dancing.

"What about me baby…where you gone take me?"
I ask innocently not really expecting an answer.

"Anywhere you wanna go Delilah, anywhere you
wanna go."
Bobby leans in and kisses me, but more
passionately than we had been doing at the juke
joint. This sealed it for me; I knew this was the
man I was to marry. I wanted to give myself to
Bobby that night, and I did. Even used some of the
tips Mable had taught me earlier in the day. The
night couldn't be any more perfect, as my life soon
would be.

8 DAISY

Two years, just as planned, Delilah married Bobby and moved out to California. But what wasn't planned was me having a baby by Joseph and moving out west myself. My baby was about to turn a year old so Joseph wanted us there, said it would be easier for him to care for us if we were in the same state. Mah May still wouldn't give in to Delilah's pleas to come to Freedomland as she calls it, but mama did agree to send my little brother J.C with me so he can stay with Delilah when Bobby be gone.

"Now when y'all get on dat train, no talking to strangers, look out fo' yo' sista and keep yo' eyes on yo' belongins. Dere's a lot of no good people out dere, slickster's and such lookin' to take what they can from folks." Mah May instructs my brother.

"And help her wit dat hollerin' baby can't nobody shut up. Ain't neva seen a baby with such a restless soul."

"Why I gotta go? Gus ain't comin'!"

J.C snaps at mama not wanting to have anything to do with California.

"Whatch yo mouth boy!! I done told you I needs one of my big boys here to help tend the fields, besides, you gone love it out west. Delilah says the sun shines most of the year, no prejudice or segregation like you go through here; a whole new life for you. Freedom to learn as much as you want, with no chains or strongholds. My baby gone breath clean, free air, taste freedom."

"I likes the south, I likes the air here."
J.C continues to object.

"Naw baby this some different air. A different kind of breathin', freedom. Mama's been chasin' it all her life. Even though they say's we free in the south, we'll live our whole lives bein' looked on as trash by people just because of the color of our skin. And I want my baby to get a chance to live as an equal for once. You hold yo head up and don't go lookin' down on folks, but don't let nobody be lookin' down on you! You's a Thomas one of God's creations! You hear me?"

Mah was holding school with J.C and I could see the lesson sinking in as he began to sit up taller and the tears became few.

"Yes ma'am, I understands."
My brother proudly answers as Mah May carefully count out some paper money and some coins she had tucked away in an old cigar box.

"Now J.C, I been savin' this money for some time now just waitin' on a special event. I can't think of a more special occasion. I done worked hard for this money, scrimpin' and savin' so be wise bout spending my last."

"Love you mama."

"Always, baby always."

J.C smiles as he places the money in his satchel along with his only two good pair of pants and enough fried chicken to get us to California.

"Daisy you and dat cryin' baby needs to hurry fo we be late."

"I's comin' mah."
But she didn't hear me she was already out tha door with J.C, Gus, and Tommy.

"Mabel be sure to tell Nate when he finishes his trainin' in Alabama, the army's got a base in Lemo, California, thas where Bobby and Joseph is stationed. Tell him to see if he can get sent there, but be sure to write us. Mama got the address."

"You thank you better than me huh?" Mabel comes out the blue with this nonsense again. Not listening to a word I just said.

"What you talkin' bout now Mabel?"

"You thank since you got that baby and Joe wanna get married, you better than me."

"Mabel I loves you, and all three of yo babies. I look up to you. You always had a man callin' on you, sometimes two or three. Always goin' to Sook's havin a good time while I sat around jes hopin' fo one man to look my way. Until Joseph came around, nobody wanted me. You don't know what its like to be the plain sista. Delilah with her beauty plus smarts, you bein' all sociable with a body I'd kill for. If Joseph wouldn't have come along, there's no telling when I woulda got a man. I loves you, we's family. Ain't you comin' out with mama if Cecil ever gets home?"

"Yeah I supposed whenever dat gone be. You kno mama ain't neva gone leave brotha out here as long as Brown gots a jail for him. But some of us might not live long enough to see California."

Mabel remarks snidely like she had a secret she ain't want nobody else to know.

"What you talkin' Mabel? I know you hidin' sumthin'. C'mon tell me, you kno I gotta go!"

"Well don't say nuthin' but Augustus bout to hit tha chittlin circuit headlinin' Big Sook's Blues Review. He gone be out 'bout six months travelin' and sangin'."

"You lie Mabel!"

"No lie."

"Maybe if it was Bassie or Ellington he was sangin' wit, but Sook…Mama gone kill him fo sho Mabel."

We hug and laugh until we both begin to cry as Mabel adores her niece one final time. We vow to never let anything or anyone come between us ever. We strengthen our sibling bond through our tears.

Mabel helps me gather my things as we join the rest of the family out front. We all walk down to the area of the tracks where the coloreds where allowed to board the train headed out west. We had to sit in the front of the train being troubled with all that smoke, but that didn't bother me and J.C not one bit, 'cause we knew freedom was just days away.

9 J.C

I had never been out of Louisiana in all my sixteen years, but was excited about what was to come. I thought about Gus most of the trip and how he was gone get away with this Big Sook thing. Gus had been leaving a lot lately, so I would have to cover for him most of the time. How he was gone continue to get away with his disappearing acts was beyond me. Soon my mind drifted from home and began to focus on what was to come. While on the train Daisy and I saw all different kinds of coloreds from all over the south, leaving they old life behind, tryna to get to Freedomland. The closer we got to California, everything changed.

"Daisy who dem folks? And what dey talking?" I ask my sista as I look at white people I don't understand.

"Quit gawking at them boy, dem what they call mesikins."

"But what they sayin'?"

"Thas how dey talk, like we talk english."

"Dey not like white folk in Louisiana, I know what they be sayin'. All white people talk like dat in California?"

"Dey's from Mesico boy not California, white folk talk regular like us out dere jes wit out tha lynchins and prejudice."

Daisy was trying to put me at ease even though she looked to be just as scared as I was. After too long Daisy was staring at the mesikin's herself until some man makes his way over trying to get Daisy's attention.

"Excuse me ma'am. If you don't mind me asking'…while are you still sitting up here in tha front?"

"Colored section mista."

"Well ma'am you are well west of the Mason Dixon, you can sit just about anywhere you like except in the conductors seat I'd imagine."
The fine spoken man chuckles removing his hat and wiping his brow with the handkerchief that was neatly folded in his left suit pocket.

   The man was tall and light-skinned with a gold tooth. Wearing a finely tailored suit with the matching hat. Daisy was trying to show the man no interest but he sat down anyway justa talking. I paid him no mind as I concentrate on the mesico strangers still tryna figure them out.

"Where bout in the south you from young lady?"

"Louisiana... How'd you know I was from tha south?"
Daisy finally taking her attention off her crying baby to hear what he had to say.

"I've taken this trip over a dozen times, and I could always spot the people from the south. They have this scared, confused look about them, like they've been startled. Me myself, I'm from Chicago going to Los Angeles to visit my uncle, I goes there may be like twice a year."

"Thas nice."

Daisy answers trying to be polite, but not showing much interest.

"Mighty fine baby you got there, sound like she gone be a sanger."

"She does have some lungs on her, I oughta know." Daisy agrees without even looking at the man.

I hope my niece's crying run him off, but he don't seem to mind. So Delilah starts fussing wit the baby trying to give the man a hint.

"Well ma'am, I think I've taken up enough of your time. So I will let you get back to caring for your baby. Good Day."
The man was gone just as quick as he had come.

"I thought he wasn't neva gone leave!" Daisy snaps shaking her head.
"Hand me my bag J.C so I can change this girl."

I hand Daisy her satchel and grab mines about to eat a piece of Mah Mays famous chicken. I loves my mama's chicken and couldn't hardly wait to eat every time she cooked it.

"It's gone!!"
Daisy panics as she buries her head deep in her satchel.

"Whas gone?" I ask Daisy as I feel around my bag for my chicken. Before she could answer I already knew what was missing, my chicken and our money!

"Joseph sent me that money to give to Delilah for lettin' us come and stay."
Daisy cries as she empties her satchel and rambles through her belongings.

"Where he go?"
I ask as I unwrap a perfectly folded cloth that was hiding a makeshift blade made fo' sneaky white California folks, but I was cutting Mr. slick wit it today.

"Put that thang up boy, das a grown man. You gone get yoself hurt." Daisy whispers through clenched teeth.

"Daisy he took my money too, he's one of those slicksters mama was talkin' bout. Mah May worked too hard for dat money and I ain't gone let nobody take it from me without a fight!"

I run off wit the knife under my shirt looking for Mr. Slick. I sweat bullets as I casually walk pass the conductor who yells that our next stop is gone be the San Francisco bay. I knew I had to hurry since this is where I would be getting off and I wasn't leaving that train without my mama's money. I finally spot Mr. Slick and I'm more nervous than before with my heart pounding out my chest. He was sitting in a box car with only two other people a few seats in front of him. He was there clutching Mah May's hard earned money, even eating her chicken. Mr. Slick was a low-down, dirty-dog and I had to do something about it.

"Scuse me Sir..."
I say, still not knowing what I'm 'bout to do. But the man looks up at me and commence to counting my money and eating my chicken in my face like I wasn't even there.

"Get out of here lil' nappy head boy and tell your sister thanks for the chicken...oh yeah, and the money."

He laughs at me putting the money in the same pocket where he had got the handkerchief from earlier. But I didn't budge.

"You heard me you little country ass Negro, get gone boy!"
Mr. Slick pushes me clear across the row into the seats next to his, just as the horn noting our arrival begins to bellow from the train. I knew if I was gone stick em' I had to do it so no one could hear. So I flew into the grown man blade first stabbing the man in unison with the horn as it continues to sound for three... four... five... more times and Mr. Slick got it every blow! His hands went limp as he reached for my neck by the third stick and he was a corpse by the final blow of the horn in Freedomland. The couple towards the front of the car didn't hear a thing; they were busy gathering their items getting ready to depart the train. Mr.

Slick grabbed at his pocket clinging' on to the money with his last breath, then nothing. I got the bloodstained money out his grasp and the rest of my chicken, racing out of there as quick as I could. Before I leave the dead man, I place his hat over his face as if he was taking a nap. I high-tailed it down the aisles of the train pushing past the people trying to depart. I finally see Daisy's face in the distance and she looks terrified.

"You get the money?" Daisy asks.

I open my hand to show her and there was the money swimming in a puddle of blood. Daisy screams and everyone turns, looking in our direction.

"It's a spider...I's sorry, I's scared of 'em." Daisy says trying to deceive the onlookers.

I throw my stuff back into the satchel and runs off the train looking for the colored only restroom, then realized I wasn't gone find one.

So I run to the restroom for men, and I see a station attendant following behind me. I hurry to one of the four stalls furthest from the door. I hear the man coming closer. He gets to my door and knocks, asking am I alright. I tell the man I was scared by this being my first time out west and it made me have to use it really bad. He believed me and finally left out the bathroom. I wrapped my hand in a piece of material I had ripped from my shirt to stop the bleeding. I walk out to see Delilah and Bobby ogling over Daisy's baby, while Daisy looking at me like she done saw a ghost.

"There's my baby brother!"

Delilah yells running in my direction. She hugs and kisses me like she hadn't never seen me before. Bobby comes over to try and help me with my bag but I keep a tight grip not allowing him to take it.

"You alright boy?"
Bobby asks me looking at my hand.

"Yes sir." I respond out of courtesy; just wanting to be left alone.

"I ain't sir, I'm your brother."

"Well, yes brother… and I'm not a boy, I'm J.C."

"I likes that, I likes that a lot. Looks like you gone fit in just fine round here."

Bobby laughs as we all load in and admire his brand new 1948 Fleetmaster. I have never seen anything like this car, and I can't even enjoy it thinking 'bout me being a killer and worst yet, what Mah May would say about me being a murderer. She always said she would not put no bad children out in the world, she rather be dead. As the train starts to announce its departure, I see's Mr. Slick still taking his eternal nap already reaching his destination. I felt bad but I knew if I hadn't stood up for me and my sister, people would be mistreating us our whole life. I had a strong feeling that this wouldn't be the last time I would have to fight for mine and what I believe in. Yeah we made it to Freedomland, but it had come at a great price, and the strange thing is, it's a price I would be willing to pay again …with no problem.

10 MAH MAY

"Where dat boy Augustus? Dat chile ain't neva home, ain't tended nan field nor fed one chicken. If it wasn't fo' old man Johnson up tha road doin' what he could, when he could, wouldn't nuthin' get done round here."
I was going on and on bout Gus to Mabel, but she wasn't paying me no mind. She just stayed focused on the peas we were shelling.

"My poor baby Thomas needs at least one of his brothers round, yo kids bout to drive him crazy. Lawd, Lawd, Lawd look at my sugar cane, need harvestin' sumthin awful. Well my grannybabe always told me that if I wanted sumthin done right I need to do it myself. I promise this place gone fall apart mo' sooner than later. I kept that boy here to help me round tha house but he's become more of a hindrance."

"Well mah, how's bout we moves out to California, It's been a year or so since Daisy and J.C left and all's you been doin is complainin' 'bout dis an dat. I thinks maybe yo soul ain't right wit yo family scattered to and fro. Cecil in jail and Nate in the army, maybe feels like you ain't in control no mo." Mable rambles trying to find her way to Freedomland.

"Well if das true, I do know who's in
control…Jehovah and thas enough for me."
I talk with Mabel a little while longer and tell her
how I just take everything to the Lord in prayer,
'*lay and leave*' and let him work it out. Just when
we was bout finish shelling all the peas, I see Gus
coming up the road totin' a paper bag, sangin and
justa snappin his fingers.

"Hey mah!"
Gus joins us on tha porch after kissing me on tha
cheek and ignoring Mabel as she rolls her eyes at
him.

"Where you been baby, you musta left mighty
early, I came to wake you but you were gone…I
have stuff I need you to do."

"Well mah, thas kinda what I wanna to talk to you
about…my duties 'round tha house."

"What about dem chile?"

"You gone need to get someone else to do em' or
maybe we could even pay somebody."

"What you talkin' Gus? I ain't got no money to be
payin folks."

I begin to rattle off the many reasons of how silly this all sounds when Gus hands me some papers he pulls out the paper bag he was carrying.

"What's this?"

"My new job, I's gone be sangin' wit Big Sook's Bl-"

"Big Sook? What you kno bout dat devil worshippin' man? Lawd tha thangs I done heard dat goes on dere, some of us know better than others."
I look at Mabel as she pays me no mind or at least act like it.

"Well mah I's been goin' dere and sangin' at night, he pays me good money. See we can pay somebody to tend to tha house and I could buy you all tha sunday-go-to-meetin' hats you want. Real big fancy ones and"

Before I know'd it I done reached back and slapped Gus, tryin to slap tha words back into his mouth. Mabel finally gets up and excuses herself into tha house.

"I have an idea who done put you up to all dis."
I eye Mabel as she closes the door.

"Mabel had nuthin to do with none of dis. Sook heard me sanging one day an asked me if I wanted to make some money. I been sanging ever since. Mama he pays me good and even bought me a uniform to perform in, look mama I want you to see it."
Before he could even get the devil glad-rags out the paper bag, I snatch it and scatter all the clothes across the grass.

"I don't wanna hear nuthin else 'bout it. Schooln' be startn' and you gone need to be getting' yo lesson. I had you sangin' in tha church since you was three years old and now you gone take that voice Jehovah done blessed you wit and waste it on some no bible believin' sinners, drunkards and whore-mongers? Lawd help my chile!"

I lay hands on Gus squeezing his head, prayn' and chantn' but Gus breaks my grip.

"Mah you actin like I'm gone be doin all those thangs."

"You lay wit dogs you get up wit fleas, you may not be drankin and fornicating now but soon… yo time will come. See how yo sista be actin', runnin' round here like she ain't got no sense."

"Well mama, I'm almost grown and I'm goin' out on tha road wit Sook."

"Well I guess you won't be livin' here whilst you doin' it."

"Well I guessin' I won't."

"Gus I done did my best to try and raise y'all, and I ain't neva had to do nuthin' fo the devil to make sure y'all ate."

"All's I wanna do is sang mama. Thas when I feels free. Delilah found freedom in California and Nate's freedom is in the army. This my freedom, I's gone be famous, make money and sang."

"Well find yo freedom elsewhere cause ain't no chile of mine gone be worshippin' tha devil unda my roof."
I leave my baby out on the porch and watch through the window as he picks up his belongings I had thrown across the yard, then he heads back up the road. I know where my baby was going, running right into Satan's arms. Lawd be a fence round my child, he gone need it.

Little was said that evening round the house, I went to bed early leaving Mabel in there feeding here chaps. I slept in the comfort of the Lord, knowing that he done already worked out the situation wit me and Gus, no worries; it's in the Lords hands now, lay and leave. Morning had come quicker than I would have liked, normally I would be up to greet the sun, but laid around until six this morning. I drop to my knees and thank the Lord for a new day, I thought a lot about Gus and the previous night, but you gotta let grown folks be grown. I was always taught that if you can't live by the house rules then you don't need to be in the house. I tie my robe and slide into my slippers and scoot across the squeaky floor boards and I notice that the door wasn't latched. My heart jumped for joy, I knew the Lord would bring my baby back to me. I knew Gus would realize how silly the whole thang was and would come home. I hurry to his room to go and talk with him when I notice the boy was still sound asleep. He was tucked all the way under the covers and I didn't have the heart to wake him so I just whispered a prayer of thanks to the Lord for bringing my baby home.

"Mama?"

I heard a voice cry out but it wasn't Gus'.

"Cecil?"
I asked just as a head appeared from under the covers.

"Cecil baby what you doin here? Brown said you'd neva see freedom as long as he was alive."

"He didn't count on his mind slippin'. Brown bout nutty as a squirrel turd. His mind totally gone. So when tha new sheriff came, he said he wasn't holding no grudges for Brown. Said that was Claxton's fault he couldn't recognize his own mare when he'd seent it, berried or not."

"Thank you Jesus!" I yell doing my holy jig which done slowed down thru the years.
 "Lawd I lose one of my boys and you bring me my other. Mama always said tha Lord don't close a door without openin' a window."

"Who gone mama? I know you say J.C out west and Nate in tha army. Who gone? Gus slept with me last night."

Just as Cecil was confused trying to figure out what was going on, Mabel comes into the room fully dressed at six in tha mornin'. She sees her brother and runs and gives him a great big hug and kiss. She must have heard what we were talking 'bout since she felt the need to join in.

"Gus ain't slept here last night, when I was leaving Sooks, Gus was curled up on tha floor sleep."

"Chile is you just getting home?"

"Well mama, see tha creek had rose last night and I couldn't cross, so I stayed tha night wit a friend til I could cross tha creek and make it home."

"Chile you ain't gotta explain nuthin to me, jes quit leavin these kids here by dem selves, spend some time wit em, they gone grow up thankin they ain't got no mammy o' pappy."

"Well Gus musta slept here then left early so he didn't have to see you mama, cuz somebody was in the bed with me last night."

"Chile quit frettin. Dat wasn't yo brother who got in bed wit you; dat was the spirits I called on to watch over my baby, dey was lookin for Gus."

"Spirits?"
Cecil and Mabel yell lookin around tha room.

"Don't pay em no mind, dey ain't gone hurt you....unlesson I ask 'em to."

GUS

"Wake up Gus; I don't be payin' you to sleep all day. My star needs to practice." I wake to Sook's kick to my legs.

"Mornin' already?" I ask as I stretch out last night's performance.

"Yeah boy, sangin dem late nights be tirin' you out, but you'll get used to it soon enough."

"Whas for breakfast?" I ask finding a wall to lean on.

 "Boy you must thank I'm Mah May or somebody. You ain't home no mo'. Round here yo either cooks for yoself or wake up wit some pretty thang to cook for you." Sook advises laughingly.

"Well, when we leavin then?"

"Soon enough star, maybe evening… here take this you won't be hungry no mo."
Sook hands me a small piece of paper bag with some powder in it.

"What's this?"

"What's this? You really is one of Mays kids. You smoke it."
Sook's laughter only confirm how green I am.

"Is it refer?"

"Nah boy, refer green like a plant. You put this in a rollie with some tobacco and smoke it. Make you feel good, won't even be hungry no more. Like magic, tha hunger disappear."

"I don't think I should."

"Fine by me, but I'll roll you one jes in case you change yo mind."
Big Sook prepares the magic stick and places it in my hand leaving me alone wit my thoughts. I walk outside and stare out past the trees that hide the juke joint from the rest of the world. I can't help but think 'bout what er'body at home was doin'. Did Mabel make it home last night or what Mah May cooked for breakfast. I was crying uncontrollably before I even realized I was crying. I knew I had to get myself under control; I couldn't let Sook see me like this. I open my hand and stare at the magic Sook had rolled me, and it was like a battle of good versus evil being up to me who would win....

"Hey, you need this?" Sook interrupts with a match for my troubles…decision made.

11 CECIL

"Mama you busy?"

I yell into the house as I sit and look at the fruits of my labor. The fields all under control, the animals fed and the cane harvested.

"Need sumthin baby?"

"Don't need nuthin mah, jes wanna talk."

"Talk? Talk 'bout what sweetie?"
Mama joins me out on the porch with two glasses of sweet tea.

"Well when I was in jail, I did a lot of prayin' and reading in my bible, and well I think I'm a preacher."

"You thinks you's a preacher? You is or you ain't baby."

"Well, I am then, at least thas what tha Lord told me when we had one of our many talks. I been savin' souls and workin' for the Lord ever since, did it the whole time I was in jail."

"Mama needs to hear you preach, did you talk to Rev. White?"

"Yes'm er'day. He been comin' to tha jail teachin' and prayin' wit me."

Mama looks unsure but proud. Not proud 'cause I was a preacher, but proud I had my own relationship with Christ, and that was priceless. She had a million questions, and I was happy to answer all of them. I begin telling mah bout my transformation when we both were stunned to see ol' Mr. Brown coming up our path wearing nothing but long handled drawers and cowboy boots carrying a rifle.

"Cecil you nigger! I know das you damn porch monkey! We's got unfinished business!"

I knew for sure Brown had really lost his mind, I look over at mama with this look of confusion about her, but she jumps right in anyway.

"Whas goin on Brown?"

"You stay outta dis May, you don't work fo' Gifton no mo', you's one of dem regular ol' niggers now!"

"And you's jes a regular ol' man now bein you ain't sheriff. Cecil done served his time leave my chile alone!"

"Brown, this me Cecil, and like I've told you fo many years, I's sorry bout yo good friend Mr. Claxton. But I was young and you know I done gave my life to tha Lord, I'mma changed man. Besides…I thought I was your friend too? We talked er'nite fo years, you seen me grow, change even unto preachin."
I start walking up on Brown trying to get him to calm down and relax that gun arm.

"You backs up nigger for I shoots you where you stands, I neva liked you!"

"Thas not true sir. Even though I was in jail, we had mighty fine times together…we did all kinds of stuff… don't you remember?"
I see Brown trying to recollect if any of what I was saying had some truth. I use the opportunity to catch em off guard by leg sweeping Brown sending him flying off his feet and the weapon soaring over his head; I catch both before they hit the ground.

"C'mon Brown, les go home." I offer the once jailer my hand and my help.

"Cecil, why you do dat to me I thought you was my friend?"
Brown asks as if I started the whole thing. He was confused as ever, as his mind continued to flip flop at will. We laugh it off as I walk Brown safely home and tell Mrs. Brown to keep a good eye on him before he hurt himself or somebody. On the way home I have to walk past one of the shacks where my daddy had been 'keepin house' wit anotha woman. It wasn't even a quarter-mile from our house. I could remember mama not wanting to come outside scared she might see daddy with his other women. I recall going to school and seeing the children of his other women all wearing new clothes and eating hot lunches while we ate on cold biscuits. The kids would tell me all the things my daddy would do for them and I would run home crying. I would try to tell Mah May but she didn't want to have no parts of nothing when it came to talking bad 'bout her husband. She didn't want to hear any of it. She loved that man, and it wasn't anything anyone could say about daddy that would have mama think one ill thing 'bout him. I vowed when I was way little dat I would neva be like my daddy. I vowed that I would take care of my family no matter what. I also taught all my brothers that the family you got at home comes first. And if they decide to have a second or third family that was fine, but never neglect yo wife and kids. I made sure my brothers understood dat, and

I promised to live every day of my life like dat, to never be like my daddy and leave my wife and kids by the wayside.

"What took so long?"
Mama asks me still a little tickled bout Brown 'cause she went on and on about the earlier events.

"Jes thinking…bout daddy mostly and partly bout California."
Mama heard what I said but only responded to the latter.

"What about California baby?"

 "I've decided I can't go."

"But we sed we's all going as a family once you came home."

"I got's my own family now Mah."

"What you talking chile?"

"I got's married two years ago, even got a set of twin boys. Sorry I didn't tell you, I never thought the need would arise since Brown vowed to keep me fo' my life time."

"Thas not the kind of thang you keep from your mama. Where da chile at?"

"She took the boys to her mama's in Georgia. She comes to visit me a few times a year. Brown would even let her stay in my cell wit me when she came to call, wasn't romantic, but we still loved each other. And mama, we didn't have relations until we was married, wanted our union to be blessed. Thas why I gotta be here when she comes to see me, she doesn't know I'mma free man. So you understand why I can't go?"

"Well baby, you know mama feels like she done got kicked by a mule. This is all so much but mama respects yo wishes. You's a grown man and you been taking care of yo self for many years. I guess it's time for me to go out west now. I been able to say I was stayin here for you and your situation but now you home I ain't got no more excuses. I assume Delilah will finally be happy that all her letters and money she been sending out here has paid off. She won... looks like I'm leavin Louisiana."

Mama walks into the house quiet and solemn like humming a hymnal. The holidays are coming and mama thought she needed to get out west and get settled soon. More so for Thomas, he was getting older and she wanted to give him a fighting chance at life on new land. Mama was able to hear me preach on her last Sunday in the south. I had finally gotten in touch with my wife and kids and they were able to spend time with mama before she left. Mah May cooked a great big Sunday dinner fit for a preacher and we all laughed and talked the whole time until Mabel started reading some of the letters Gus had sent. The family was enjoying em', but mama wasn't. She never read any of Augustus' letters. Mabel was happy to open and read em' since Gus would always put money in the letters. Mama didn't want to have nothing to do wit Gus, the letters the money nor the pleas for forgiveness. Mama's life was about to change and she with it. The spiritual warrior born and bred in the south was about to be plucked out of her comfort and tossed into the unknown. But my mama is strong, one of the strongest women I know and she always taught me to walk by faith and not by sight, and I'm sure she will be taking some of her own advice this time around.

12 NATHANIEL

"Woman give me my bottle!" I demand from the girl I just paid to be my entertainment for the night.

"You ain't sharing' pilot boy?"

She laughs prancing round in panties and my army hat.

"I pay you for what I want, so you needs to pay me for what you want."
I snatch my bottle and guzzle the remaining shine and lays back down dropping the bottle to the floor.

"Private Thomas is you drunk already?
My bunky Private Johnson asks after he finishes up with his girlfriend.
 "You know what the Sgt. said about staying out, getting drunk and messing wit loose women, he sed lots of 'em got diseases and such."

"Ain't nuthin this pretty, dat dirty."
I tell my bunky as my entertainment is now on my lap trying to squeeze a little more booze out my bottle agreeing with my last statement.

"C'mon soldier."
Johnson helps me up and tries to make me as presentable as possible with no luck. We get back to base and that's the last thing I remember.

"Nate…Nate! Wake up!"

I faintly hear Johnson but my body ain't responding. The next thing I know I was jolted by an open-handed wake-up to the face.

"What the hell man? Why you hit me?"
I sit up ready to clock Johnson in the eye.

"Man serge just left from trying to wake you up. He said he was tired of this and wanted to see you immediately, told us not to wake you, but I couldn't let you sleep any longer, I didn't want you to get into more trouble than you already are."

"Thanks man, was he very upset?"

"Was he? He was steaming demon! You know, I think this is it. I don't think you will be able to talk him out of this one."

"You know I'm the one with tha golden tongue. I could talk my way out of anything. I'll be alright, I'mma go in there and straighten all this out right now. Betta take me a shower first."

I hop in the cold water in hopes that it would put some life back in me but also to hide my tears as I had no idea how to spin this to the sergeant. I had used any excuse of substance on past antics and was all out of reasonable defenses. I hurried over to the sergeant's quarters with reluctant haste to await my fate. I walk in to my superior smoking a cigar dawning a look of disgust and my stomach begins to churn and bubble as I look for a seat finding none available. Serge took no time for formalities and jumped right in my ass. I really wanted to be attentive and receive my scolding but last night was coming back to haunt me in a major way. I struggle to raise my hand in an effort to request some water but was shut down immediately.

"Not one word Private Thomas! You are an embarrassment to the uniform, my platoon and the United States Army! You run sleeping with anything with a skirt and dranking up everythang but water! You leaves me no choice but to discharge you dishonorably immediately. You can pack your personal items and take everything else issued by the U.S Army to the clerk who will give you your walking papers. Stop by medic, they've been looking for you since Friday…good writtens!!"

I opened my mouth to plea my case and at that moment became violently ill and left last night right there on his feet and floor. I could feel the steam coming out of the sergeant's ears warning me that there was nothing left to say. I turn to leave the room wondering what medic could possibly want with me, but the United States Army had one last official duty for me and serge handed me a mop.

GUS

"...u got me whirlin' oohh girl, you me twirlin'...ooo"

Whenever I would sing, I would have all the women swooning over me and the men would be going crazy over my background singers.
From Louisiana to Chicago on up to New York, Big Sook's blues review was bringing down the house everywhere we went. We played dives, juke joints and some nice halls, but wherever we played, I did just what I told my mama I was gone do, sang and make lots of money. And this performance in Little Rock would be no different.

"Baby Gus and the Gustines will be back after a fifteen minute break!"
Sook announces as the crowd starts booing, all mad because they wanted more me and they wanted me now.

"I sholl like yo' songs." One of my well-endowed female fans compliments as she stops me and flashes her titties as I head out back.

"Yeah, I don't know why they calls you baby Gus, looks all man to me." A different lady adds.

All us Thomas boys are tall, clearing at least six feet with dark complexions. I had the height but not the color. My complexion had come from my daddy's side of the family giving me the fine hair and fair skin, the women thought I wore a konk but was even more impressed when they found out my hair was all natural, with just a touch of pomade. So the ladies loved Gus and I loved the ladies.

"Ladies excuse me, but I'm trying to get something for my thirst, I'm parched." I croon needing any excuse to get out back.

"You can have my drink Baby Gus."
The well-endowed lady offered up her moonshine by pouring it down her titties for me to lap up.

"Sorry baby, don't drank no booze."

"Hey buddy c'mere and let me talk to you for a second." My friend and drummer D. Jenkins swoops in and rescues me like he has to do every night if I wanna get a break. We laugh as we make it out back of the club with no more interruptions.

"Man them ladies know they love them some Gus. Boy sooner or later you gone have to start paying me for saving your butt."

"Forget all dat...Where's tha magic?"
I asked trying to get straight to it before it's time for me to go back on stage.

"I got it right here, this time I rolled it wit some good refer I got from a cracka in Georgia. Slow down, it ain't' going nowhere."
I snatch the stick out of D's hand, fire up and let the magic begin.

"How you gone tell me how to do my own shit, I pays for it, I smokes it when I want to. But damn Dee… this is some good shit."

"Enough Mr. Star Man, you still got to be able to perform, don't get too high."

"Don't worry 'bout me, the magic helps me do my best work…let's go. I'm ready now."
I tuck away the rest of my secret love until after the show.
"Man you ain't gone let me get some of that?"
Dee asks with a tinge of hostility in his voice.

"My drugs, my way. Here take this money and get me some more for tonight, more refer too. I might even share with you this time."
I laugh and stumble a little bit as I enter the back of the club.

"You gone be alright man?"
Dee asks me while tucking the cash away.

"Ain't I always?"

I straighten up heading back in the club and hits the stage. The crowd is going crazy, ready to finish partying the night away. I barely make it to my microphone, when I start seeing double and begin to feel like I was floating above the band. This was it. This is why I love the magic and it loves me. It takes me on journeys a woman neva could. With the magic I was king and unstoppable. I was on top of the world and nothing was gone bring me down. Not now, not eva! The magic doing what it does and has neva let me down yet and tonight would be no different. Just when I finally get my bearings about myself, some man in the audience starts heckling me every time I open my mouth to sing. The man is saying something I can't understand until the music stops allowing the whole club to hear what this man's rant is all about.

"You no good so-in-so, you slept with my wife you whore-monger! I shoulda whipped yo ass back in Georgia, but I'mma get yo pretty ass tonight!"

The crazed man charges the stage not worrying 'bout the boo's and trash being tossed at him from the crowd. As he reaches the stage, he trips on his way up the stairs but was snatched up from behind by a man from the crowd before he even reaches the ground. The stranger commences to whipping the trouble-makers ass all through the crowd not showing any mercy. The crowd cheers and chants, "Joe Louis!" as the hero of the night stands over his knocked-out opponent. I jumped into the crowd to show my gratitude to the Good Samaritan and was taken back when I got close enough to hear the drunken man's ramblings.

"Don't you ever threaten my brother or come to one of his shows again in your life!!"

"Nate? Nate Thomas?"

The man turned and just as I suspected it was my big brother, pissy drunk. He collapses in my arms; D. Jenkins and I carry him outside to give him some air. We barely made it out as the crowd was angry that I was once again taking a break. Even Sook tried to make me get back on stage, but I need to take care of Nathaniel first.

"Nate what you doin' in Huntsville you supposed to be in Tuskegee?" I ask confusingly.

"Me and Uncle Sam didn't get along to well, but me and Cletus is best buddies." Nate mumbles, slobbing on both of us.

"Cletus? Who dat?"

"Das my bootlegger, he takes mighty good care of me." Nate advises while feeling his pockets, looking for something.

"Awe, naw Nate don't tells me you done got yoself kicked out the Army for drankin?"

"Put it like this…I dranks and I ain't in the army no more."

"Here brother smoke this, it will make you feel good instantly, like magic." I offer knowing it wasn't right but the magic was the only thang that made me feel better when times became too much to bear. I hand him the rest of the stick I was smoking on earlier.

"Whas this Gus?"

"Gone head, gone make you feel good…real good."

"Oh Lawd! Gus you ain't wit dat is you? Not my little brother!!"

Nate begins to cry uncontrollably I think it's more so from the booze and not from the news of me and the magic.
"C'mon brother, times are changing, loosen up."
I try to assure Nathaniel its okay, but his crying got worst.

"O.K… Look Nate I put it up…see, its gone. You can stop cryin'. Brother, you can't be dat upset over a little partyin'."

"Gus I'm dyin'."

"Dying?"

"Well I feels like I am … they say's I got sumthin called Sivless, says you gets it from sleeping wit nasty women."

"Sivless? You been sleeping wit nasty women?"

"Gus I been sleeping with all kinds of women. When the army was about to kick me out they said I was ill, and told me about a program for men sick like me, so I signed up."

"Is you scared?"

"Why should I be? The program is ran by the U-ni-ted-States of this here America, gets no better than good ol' Uncle Sam, no better hands to be in."

Nate slumps down to the ground finally locating what he had been searching for pulling a swig size bottle of shine out his back pocket while I stare at my brother with tears streaming down my face. I was looking at a man who wasn't well and was thirty pounds lighter than he was one year ago. I sit next to my brother and smoked the rest of the magic I had stashed. Nate offered the bottle and even though I don't drink I accept. The first drink of my life would be shared with my ill brother; I only pray it won't be our last.

13 MAH MAY

"I miss Louisiana mama."
My baby Thomas confesses as I prepare him for his first day of school in California.

"Why you ain't even gave it a chance baby."

"People too nice and I can beat all da kids in the sportin games here. Besides, they makes fun of my name...Thomas Thomas."

"Why I thanks it's a beautiful name and none of that is a reason not to like California. Mama sure you gone make lots of friends. This what they calls hi-school, you graduate in three years and then go off to college like yo sista Delilah did."

"Really mah? I can play ball too?"

"All year round. They got football, basketball, baseball teams, could even run if you wanna...you likes to run. See you can do anything and er'thang you done dreamt bout, jes like when you used to listen to Sweetwater playin ball for dat New York team...dat could be you baby."

"Sweetwater Clifton?" Thomas beams.

"Yeah baby, you could do that and so much more. Mama moved you out here so you can dream yo dream of freedom. See Delilah found her's in her civil rights groups, traveling and opening chapters all over the country. Your sister Daisy's freedom is in her family and catering business, your big brother J.C just loving the freedom to make all the money he wants building houses and running round with all those pretty girls. Everybody has they own dream of freedom, and California allows us with the Lords will to make those dreams come true."

"I wanna play football and be famous!"

"And you can too. You can do anything your heart can dream up. Next week we gone ride to San Francisco and pick up Cecil, the church got some things for him to do out here, so you tells him all about it, I'm sure he'd love to hear yo' dreams."

"Alright mama. And mama, I loves California, but not more than you. Love you."

"Always, baby, always."

Tommy hugs me on his way out the door and was in better spirits than he was when he had woke this morning. Thomas was the biggest all my boys. They were all tall, but Tommy was solid muscle.

He stood six foot three and was hovering around two-hundred pounds. He beat the average grown man at any kind of sport and was swift at anything he did. The boy was fast. I knew if anyone of my boys could play sports and become famous at it, it would be my baby. There was nothing Tommy couldn't do with a ball. He said he liked California, but I know he missed Nate and Gus. It's been close to two years and I have to admit that I missed them too. Lately I was feeling sorta like a tugging at my soul, like sumthin wasn't right wit them two. Gus wrote often but I never cared to read any of the letters, Mabel even quit reading the letters after Gus stopped putting money in the envelopes. Last she read was that Gus saw Nate in Huntsville said he was ill, maybe even dying. I blame myself for leaving Louisiana and not staying and waiting for my babies to come home. I pick up one of Gus' letters and read it finally after all this time. I cry like I lost some kin. I cry for my babies and for myself. Gus said he was finish with the review and he wouldn't come out west understanding how I couldn't love sinners like him and Nate no more. He even sent me his last twenty dollars. I put the money in a envelope with another twenty and sent it back to my baby. I could try to make it right with my boys if the Lord allows me the chance, and if he doesn't all I can do is ask him to have mercy on their souls as well as mine.

GUS

I could hear Cecil and some woman arguing as I
walk up the steps to my family's Louisiana house.
After everything me and mama done been through
I still can't believe I'm able to come home. I
almost turn and walk away ashamed, but I know I
have nowhere else to go. I try to wait out the
argument but it seems never ending.

"Cecil when you coming back?" I hear the lady
ask my brother through her tears.

"When the Lords work is done. Barbara, the
church needs a preacher until they pastor gets
better, he's taken ill. When I makes enough money
I'll send for you and the boys."

"We can come now, my mama will give us tha
money." Barbara pleads.

"Ya mama barely eatin' as-is, besides, where y'all
gone stay?"

"I guess you right, I jes don't know what I'm
gonna do without you. What do I know about

tendin' fields and such; I guess I could get one of the neighbors to help."

"Or I could." I offer as I walk in to the house, or hobble rather being that the cast on my leg doesn't give me much room movement.

"Gus Thomas!"
Cecil blurts outs running to hug me, but not knowing where to grab me since I had casts and bandages covering most of my body.

"Boy what done happened to you?"

"Let's just say a woman happened, well her husband happened…long story Cecil."

"Told you 'bout messing wit married women long time ago, ain't no need to with all the single women runnin' round. I knew sumthin bound to happened to ya, the Lord want you to find yo' own wife, be with her or by yourself."

Cecil continues to preach bout marriage and fornicating turning the home coming into a mini-sermon.

"I forgot you a preacher now, sholl sound like one…and you get my sinners stamp of approval."

"I need you to get serious now, I'm going out west for a spell to see mama and them, I wants you to care for my family 'til I return. Gus, this is all I gots and I'm trusting you with it, my home, my wife and my family."

"Brother, I promise when I gets better I will handle everything and more. Don't worry about nuthin."

I look over at Barbara, she drops her head as we make eye contact and she leaves the room. Cecil and I talk all evening reflecting and catching up on family ongonings. Barbara didn't came back out, so I never got to know her before Cecil left, leaving us in a strange way. I had suffered from a lot of evil weaknesses and addictions through the years, women being the worst. As I look at Barbara, all I can do is pray that the ass whooping the last lady's husband put on me cured me of at least that demon.

14 Gus

When Cecil left Louisiana Barbara and I were complete strangers, but after two years we are damn near husband and wife, without the sex. We do everything together. As a family we take care of the house and raise the kids. Barbara even helps me write songs and accompanies me when I sing some nights. All this with nothing but empty promises and letters from Cecil. He tells Barbara he will be to get her soon enough. He says the pastor has passed away and he can't take the time to make the trip. Cecil writes that the church gave him a home to live in as long as he stayed and remained their pastor. He always promises he would be back, in every letter he has sent for the past six months… Barbara was finally fed up.

"Not even five dollars in the letter!" Barbara complains after reading one of Cecil's many fairy-tales she'd received.

"Well maybe he forgot, 'sides, we ain't hurtin' fo' no money. Sook pays me good for the songs I write for the artist on his record label. We gone be alright"

"Don't you mean the songs *we* write?" Barbara jokingly remarks, while not joking.

"Boys y'all go to bed while I talk to Uncle Gus for a spell."

The boys hop up and do as told, as I sit and wonder what Barbara has on her mind. I hope she ain't got another pity-party planned for herself; I'm tired of being invited to those. As she helps the boys gather their things I notice how fine she is. All that undefiled womanliness going to waste. Barbara quietly joins me not knowing the thoughts that I'm trying to put out my head, but once again I'm unsuccessful as Barbara was too beautiful.

"Gus... you like me?"

"Of course I like you, you my brother's wife. Why you askin' Barbara?"

"Well honestly I don't believe Cecil is comin' back, and I been missing the touches of a man. I thought since we was living together anyway maybe we could..."

"We could be together." I jump in finishing her sentence.

"It's just a suggestion; we could do it one time maybe and nuthin more."

"Well Barbara, I guess I shoulda told you long ago, but I don't think Cecil is comin' back either, he done started anotha family out west, with one of the members of the church, she even with child now from what I hear."
Barbara breaks down crying just as I thought she would, that's why I never told her. I didn't decide to tell her to hurt her; I just don't want her to feel guilty if anything was to happened between us.

"How are they letting a cheating, whore-monger be pastor?"

"Thas another thing, he not the pastor, he's a Jackleg."

"A jack what?"

"A jackleg, thas a man who preaches but doesn't have his own church."

"I knew sumthin wasn't right with his letters. So what of us? I need you now more than ever."
Barbara tells me but shows me even better by caressing my family jewels.

"You sho this what you wants to do? You know we can't undo it once it's done."

"Never been more sure."

I undress Barbara and take her, all of her and give her all of me. It's as if we just had our wedding night after years of dating. After the deed was done, we decided we would share a bed, raise the twins as husband and wife not mama and uncle, hell they already had my last name. Months pass and things couldn't have been better, we woulda forgotten all about Barbara's real husband if the twins didn't look so much like him. Cecil still sent the letters saying he was coming, but up 'til now hadn't proved to be a man of his word.

"Listen Gus, you hear dat?"
Barbara asks me in the middle of us making love as we did nightly for the past two years.

"Jes tha wind girl, no worries. Hush now you messing up my stroke."
I tell Barbara not missing a beat but was stopped mid-pump by a blunt object to the head.

"You damn Jezebel!" Cecil yells "And my own brother taking my wife!"

I stand there trying to defend my actions with all my business dangling for the world to see.

"Cecil, it's been years and you done took up with a another woman even taking care of her kids out west, not even taking care of your own. I'm these boys pappy, I feed and clothe these kids. What you thank she was gone do, be like mama? Neva be with anotha man again in life?"

"I came to bury Nate."
That's all Cecil could say through all of what had just transpired.

"I was comin' to get Barbara and bring her out west when I got word about Nate. I wanted to see what you wanted to do Barbara, come with me, go with yo mama…whatever you choose at this point."

"You had no such plans to come and get me!" Barbara explodes. "All those years you fed me all dat horseshit bout yo daddy and how he left y'all poor and hungry while he took care of other women and they children. You always promised you would never do nothing like that. But congratulations, you done turned into your daddy. And now you wanna sends me back to my mama with two kids and no man, I don't think so…I'm staying here with Gus and we gone start us a family."

"Well Barbara," I interrupt after putting some clothes on my ass. "I thinks I'm goin' back to

California with Cecil being Nate dead an all. Ain't nuthin left out here for me."

"You wanna leave me too? You no good whore-mongering sinners, how could y'all do this to me? Gus after all we been thru, how could you do this?"

"Blood thicker than mud." I remind Barbara as Cecil and I go outside and make our plans to go to Alabama.

"You know she's right."
Cecil says not really wanting to speak about the unspeakable.

"Right about what?"

"About me turning into what I despise... daddy. She has a point, everything he did to us, I did to them. Its funny how life will lead you down a road you thought you tried so hard to stay away from." We talked all night, I don't think either one of us slept a wink. We left as planned early that morning on our way to lay our brother to rest and bury the shame that had died along with him. Once we placed Nate in the ground, we never spoke of him again. We eventually got word that Nathaniel had fathered a child before his demise, but we didn't know how true it was since we never saw a baby.

We didn't even feel it was a need to tell Mah May, once we got back in California. We let her mourn her deceased son and eventually she was able to enjoy all seven of her remaining children being on the same coast for the first time in a long time. When we came out west, we pretty much took the town by storm. My sisters had already made a name for the Thomas' and us boys came in making an even bigger statement. J.C branched out starting his own construction company, even recruiting me and Cecil as partners. Delilah was living her dream as she rose through the ranks of the NAACP traveling across country wearing the finest of clothes and furs speaking at different conventions throughout the U.S. She and Bobby became a highly influential black couple when it came to black culture and politics. Delilah finished school when she arrived in California graduating from UCLA giving her diverse, lifelong connections that she still uses to this day. Bobby finances all of Delilah's endeavors thanks to the U.S Army and their compensation for him being a faithful soldier for many years well past the war. Daisy Mae's, The Delectable Daisy was the hottest eatery in town thanks to her older siblings top shelf connections. Daisy catered the classiest events up and down California and had the best food in town, bringing that southern touch to the west coast. Then there was Mabeleen. She hadn't found her nitch in life, but lived it just the same. I thinks ain't much she can do if Mah May ain't got sumthin to do with it. So they stayed hitched to one another whether the other one liked it or not. Mable never had to work a day in her life, but never went without. We all loved our nieces and nephews and made sure Mabel and her babies didn't have a care in the world. Sometimes I think Mabel took advantage of that, but one thing I can say about my sister is that she gone get what she wanted whether it was given to her willingly or not.

15 MAYBEL

"Where Daisy at?"
I ask Joseph as I hand him the things Mah May asked me to drop off to him.

"At the eatery, don't get here 'til late. She needs to hurry home, I like to eat too. She thank since I'm her husband and not a paying customer I have to wait to eat."

"I's cook you sumthin, what you liking?"

"What I'm wanting from you Mabel can't be cooked on no stove."

"We can't keep sneakin' round like dis Joseph, sumbody bound to find out."

"If you really wanted to stop you wouldn't be here."

"Mah sent me here drop off some stuff and pick up the laundry so she could wash it being Daisy so busy an all."

"See thas what I'm talking 'bout, she always so busy, always gone never got time for me. I's a man, I needs to feel like a man. I feel like a child with no mama."

"You's far from a child I can vouch for that, can't no child do the things you do to me."

"C'mere girl, remind me I'mma man, your man."

"Joseph you's bad and ain't ever gone be right."

CECIL

I told you boys I ain't paying another red cent!" The white property owner informs me after we done started constructing this state of the art office complex.

"Didn't you sign the contract agreeing to pay a total of five thousand not including material?" I pull out the contract showing the oakie his signature next to J.C's.

"Nigger, dat paper don't mean shit to me, I told you boy's I'll give y'all twenty-five hundred and y'all gone take it! Damn niggers think because they let that monkey Jackie Robinson play on the field with white folks y'all can do whatever you want. Damn niggers!"

"I got your nigger, cracka. This ain't the south, and we will be getting all our money… today. Shut it down boys!! Don't swing not one more hammer, don't hit not one mo' nail!!" I command the Thomas Construction company workers to stop working until we get the rest of our money.

"Y'all gone finish my building, I gots a deadline to meet!!"

The redneck jumps in my face swearing and cursing up a storm, but I pay him no mind, this made the man even madder. As he continued on his tirade we laughed our asses off making the situation worse. The other white workers that were on the worksite decide to come to the rescue of the property owner trying to intimidate us into getting back to work. Things were looking bad and was about to turn ugly when Gus and J.C finally pull up, hopping out the car running to see what was going on.

"Why ain't nobody working? What the hell's happening Cecil?" J.C asks but looking at the property owner.

"This man say he only gone pay us half the agreed price not the original amount so I told everybody to stop working 'til we get our money!"

"How much he done paid already?"

J.C asks sizing up the cracker giving him another once over.

"He done paid fifteen hundred dollars so far, not including money for materials, and by the way he acting, I don't think he gone pay us at all."

"You damn right nigger! I ain't giving y'all shit and you gone finish..."

Before he could get another word out his mouth J.C knocks the shit out the oakie starting an all-out riot on the job site. The white boys were no match for us, we tore they asses up sending them retreating to thieir trucks. J.C jumps on top of a pallet of bricks and yells, "TEAR THIS SHIT DOWN!!"

And we were happy to do so, when we finished there wasn't nothing standing, that included all the other work the white plumbers and electricians had done been working on. We laugh as we were 'bout to load up and go home, but J.C wasn't finished. He went up to the oakie with his Baby Browning in hand, and told him he owed him another thousand dollars for the materials he made him demolish. The white man emptied his pockets and ran, but J.C only took what was owed to him, joined me and Gus in his 1952 Chevy and we rode off laughing in the crackers face. Taking no loses, was our motto. We never worried about getting' in trouble since we were close friends with judges, police chiefs and attorneys all over town.

"Boy you see the look on dat cracker face when you knocked him on his ass?" Gus asks J.C as we ride home listening to Billie Holiday flowing thru the speakers singing our cares away.

"He didn't know what hit em', I wretched all the way back to Louisiana on dat one." J.C and Gus continue to laugh but I didn't think any of this was funny.

"I think this gone be my last day working with y'all." I felt this was the time to get out; I needed to tell them eventually.

"What you talking 'bout Cee?" J.C pulls over to the side of the road to see what was wrong with me.

"You know we got the big contract to build the new church, they done paid a lot of money so far, and we can't let em down."

"Thas just it, the church is why I need to quit. The word is that they considering me for pastoral-ship."

"Don't you gotta be married for something like dat?" JC snarls through the rear view mirror.

"I am married."

"I mean married to the woman you living with not some woman two-thousand miles away." J.C snaps.

"I'm gone take care of all that, but I just know I can't be out here street brawlin' like some hoodlum then up in the pulpit on Sunday mornings."

"Fine by me," J.C says as he starts the car up and pushes his way back into traffic.
 "Seem to me like fighting the least of your problems, needs to be worryn bout them two families you jugglin'. And as for the brawling, let me tell you sumthin Cecil and don't you ever forget it, I ain't never took nothing from nobody I

didn't earn and I'll be damned if I let someone take shit from me…Pastor Thomas!"

I could tell J.C was mad but I needed to do what was going to best for me and *all* of my families. The ride home was quiet and once we pulled up in front of my house, I tried to explain to my brothers but they didn't want to hear it and pulled off. I stood there listening to the laughter coming from inside my home. I had a family who truly loved me here and a family that hated me thousands of miles away. I knew I had to get Barbara to California in order for things to be right with me and the Lord, but it's gonna have to wait until I'm ordained pastor of Faith Foundation Missionary Baptist Church. *Pastor Thomas*, I likes the sound of that.

16 MAH MAY

"Boy why dat man keep calling here for you? I thought you was through with dat mess years ago?"
I confront Gus as soon as he gets in from work.

"Who you talking 'bout Mah?"

"Big Sook. Man keep callin er' hour on the hour talking bout it's important, it was sumthin bout dat man I neva liked." I admit to Gus as I fix him a plate of greens, fried chicken and hot water cornbread.

"He leaves a number mama?"

I point Gus over to the phone, and he ignores his dinner to make his call all excited like a child on Christmas. Gus stayed on tha phone talking and laughing for over an hour. When I brought him his reheated plate he had some things he wanted to talk about, so I joined my baby to see what was on his
mind.

"How Sook doing? Did he call to say 'hey' or did he call to tell you he was opening anotha heathen-haven and he wants you to headline?"

"Well Mah Samuel is fine, and no, he ain't opening no juke joints, matter of fact he did call to say *hi* and also tell me he found the Lord."

"The Lord wasn't lost son, he was."

"Well, he say he's starting a gospel label and he wants me to make a record. He know'd thas where my roots was at anyway. This is it mah, I'm back!"

The flesh wanted to be excited for my baby, but for some reason my soul wouldn't allow it. I didn't want to question Sook's new found relationship with Christ, that's between him and the Lord, but I know my child has demons, many demons and the thangs that could happened to him playing with the Lord, I dread to think about. But now my baby wanted a reaction, he wants his mama to be proud of him, he wants my approval.

"That's good son." I unconvincingly answer.

"That's all you have to say? What, you don't believe sinners can become saints?"

"Baby, mama ain't got no heaven nor hell to put nobody in, it don't matter what I think, it's what's in your heart."

"Mama, all I wanna do is sang, that's all I ever wanted to do. And this time I'll be sangin' for the Lord. Now you can be happy for me or not but this is what I'm gonna do. I'll be leaving for Chicago next week, to cut my first album."

"What about the company? What's J.C gone say?"

"Thas J.C's company, he does what he wants to do anyway, he ain't gone miss me. But you mama, I want you to be happy for me. I know I done did some things that made you shame of me at times, this is my chance to make it up to you... make you proud of me for once."

"Mama's always been proud of you, just disappointed at times."

"Mama thas why I love you."

"Always, baby, always." I shake my head and know that out of all my children, Gus was my most adventurous. As twins, Gus and J.C couldn't be more different.

J.C was focused and didn't mind some hard work, as to where Gus would do things at a drop of a hat, and wasn't scared to fall flat on his face; he would just dust himself off and try again. I put him in

Jehovah's hands long ago, and there he will stay, lay and leave. Maybe by him going to Chicago, he will decide to move there, because the house was starting to get too crowded. Delilah gave me this home after Bobby bought her a brand new house to fit the lifestyle they were blessed to be living. But now that Gus is here, we gone need more room. Once Thomas finishes college, he will get his own place, but until then he wants his room left untouched, even when he's off at school, he expects no one to be sleeping in his room. Big ol' baby. Tommy made me promise that he would buy me a new house if I only do that one thing for him. All my babies had dreams, and chased after them, I just worry 'bout my Mabel. She knows she likes her some men. And none of her children are babies no more so she goes and comes as she pleases. Stays gone the entire weekend at times. Lord knows I prays for that child to find her a man, a real man, her own man. My thoughts were interrupted by Daisy calling saying she was stopping by like she did every evening on her way home from work, if for no other reason but to reflect on her day. I had a close bond with all my children, but my baby girl stayed under me more than any of the seven.

"Hey mama." Daisy enters carry a pot and a crystal cake plate.

"Hey baby, what ya got there? Let me guess, it's Sunday so you got…gumbo and red velvet cake."

"You got it mah! Thought I'd come sit with you for a spell."

"Ain't you gotta get home to your family chile?"

"Not tonight, the kids at Delilah's house and Joseph's out of town. He been doing a lot of traveling lately. Been gone 'bout every weekend this past month."

"Gone where? For what?"

"I don't know mama, just say's for work or none my business when I ask. B'sides, I be busy anyway, I ain't got time to be worrying myself with all that nonsense."

This didn't sound right, and I know my baby has only been in one relationship, so she might not think nothing's wrong with their union.

"Now don't get mad at mama, but is er'thang alright with your marriage? Have y'all been having problems lately?"

"I don't know mama, he be fine one day, then all yelling the next bout I'm never home and I don't care 'bout him and how I needs to be more of a wife and mother."

"Well do you agree? What do you think about what he sayin'?"

"I be all confused like mah. At times I see what he's saying, but then I realize I'm living my dream doing something I love, and making good money. It seems as if nothing I do makes Joseph happy any more so I just decided to focus on my children."

"Baby just take it to the Lord, trust and believe. Not only will the Lord answer your call, he'll order your steps. Now hand me that cake."

I hug my baby and try to comfort her soul. I let her know that everything will be alright, because she's a child of God. We pray, laugh and leave our worries in the burgundy, velvety goodness when Mabel finally comes home drunk as a skunk joining us at the table. She doesn't say a word just rakes her finger along the frosting of Daisy's cake, and slams it in her mouth.

"Welcome home stranger."
I say but gets no response from Mabel her sensing the sarcasm in my tone.

"Taste alright, needs more cream cheese."

Mabel slurs, smacking on the icing.

"You decided to come home I see."

"Mama is there a problem with us living here because we can go? I could get my own place."

"No Mabel, I ain't said you gots to leave, but if you must, fine by me, you can go…sick and all."

"I ain't sick, I'm just fine."
Mabel snaps as she begins coughing up phlegm then spits it in a napkin she snatches from Daisy.

"You needs to rest sister."

"I gets plenty of rest, don't worry 'bout dat. All I do is rest when I ain't *here*."
Mabel smirks helping herself to a piece of Daisy's cake.

"Das whas wrong wit ya, always wanting something that don't belong to you." I snap. Daisy may not know what's going on, but I see right through Mabel and Bobby's mess.

"Maybe you right mama." Mabel laughingly answers as she excuses herself from the table and begins to head up stairs but not before she stops and turns to Daisy,

"Daisy?"

"Yeah Mabel?"

"Tell your husband I says *hi*."

17 CECIL

"Glory, Glory....Hallelujah...since I laid my burdens down..."

The churches combined choirs sing songs of praise as the twelve hundred member congregation has its first worship service at the new site for the Faith Foundation Missionary Baptist Church with Rev. C.W. Thomas as pastor. I sit in the plush pulpit surrounded by six jacks and look out at my Parishioners. My whole family is in attendance and I could see that mama was proud as can be. I think back on how far we'd came from coming up poor, to some of the more prominent citizens of the times...white or black. Thomas was also happy because he loved the young women hanging all around him, they knew he would be playing professional football soon, and was hoping he was looking for a wife. J.C was being complemented and praised for his company building the biggest church in the valley and maybe even in the state to date. This made J.C the most eligible bachelor in his age group. But good-luck ladies, because none of my brothers were interested in settling down yet. But my sisters were an entirely different story as they sat in their furs thanking the Lord for this day with their husbands by their side. Mabel just sat there looking annoyed, like she had somewhere to go and only came because Mah May made her. But not even Mabel could spoil this day. This was a blessing long time coming. I close my eyes and meditate as Gus finishes up the B selection he was leading with the choir. As I take my place in the pulpit, I see Mah May cringe when Gus announces he would be selling his new gospel album out by his car after church.

"Thank you brother for that announcement. Now church we done sent up praises with the choir, it's time to get fed. Time for the word. I know today is a day of giving thanks to the Lord for blessing us with such a beautiful building to help uplift the kingdom of God, but this morning I would like to speak on a subject a little off topic. So would you please stand and turn to Ephesians chapter 5:25 and we will read through verse 33. I give the congregation time to find the passage and I realize why the Lord put this on my heart to be my message. I knew this had to be addressed eventually, and I needed to face it head on. Lately I had been praying asking the Lord to give me the strength to drink from this cup when the time arises. As I begin to read the text, the back doors of the church fly open and a lady carrying a baby with 3 other children following behind her push past the ushers and marches to the front of the church making the deacons make room for her and her group. It wasn't until the woman had gotten close to her seats that I realized it was Barbara and the twins. My pause and stare was so dramatic the entire church turned to see who was walking up the aisle. I gather myself from the shock and stumble my way through the sermon. The remaining part of service went off without any problems and after benediction I managed to avoid my California family, making my way over to Barbara and her clan. Augustus had beat me there and was holding the baby Barbara was carrying with a strange look on his face.

"Afternoon Barbara."
I greet, not knowing what else to say.

"Cecil." she responds not making eye contact.

"When you arrive?"

"Last night, thought I'd surprise you... surprised?"

"Yes I am. C'mere boys give me a hug."

The two boys only move after they mama give them the okay. I hug them and it is cold and not returned. I kind of understand what they were feeling, they weren't babies anymore and at this age they knew exactly what was going on between me and they mama.

"Who's this pretty gal?" I turned to the overly developed young lady who had a familiar look about herself as she was checking out the groups of boys throughout the church.

"Oh that there is your niece, Nathalia… Nates daughter."

I reach out and hug her so tight I scare the poor child, I cry because I wasn't sure if the child even existed and would have never imagined I would be seeing her face to face. I thought once I laid my brother to rest, that was the end, but now I see it's the beginning of a different part of him.

"And who's this strapping young man?" I ask as I take the baby from Gus who had the same intimate look as the older girl.

"Oh dat there my boy." Barbara proudly confesses as she adjusts the small child's clothes which were a little tussled. But the news sent me in a rage.

"What you talkin' Barbara? You done went and had a child with some strange man while I was gone?"
I had raised my voice loud enough for the remaining members that hadn't exited the church could hear.

"No stranger," she says calmly taking the baby out my arms and places him back on Gus' lap.

"This here yo nephew… Gus his daddy."

I look over at Gus and now know why he had that confused look on his face. Before I knew it I had snatched Barbara up by the arm as Cora runs up and asks what was going on.

"Oh you must be my wife-in-law."
Barbara says to Cora as she rips her arm from my clutch.

"What is she talkin' bout Cecil? I don't know this woman!"

"Cora, this here is my wife Barbara and my twin boys."
I drop my head in shame but not before Cora was able to get in a slap. I was so mad at myself because I had all the time in the world to work this out and because of me, Cora got hurt.

"Cecil, in all these years you could have told me, you had had me thinking the reason you didn't want to marry me was for something I was doing. You made up every excuse you could not to get married and now you big preacher man, so you move your wife and children out west. What about us? We're your family too!"

"No need to be worrying 'bout all dat Cora." Gus stands up with the baby on his hip finally saying something through the commotion.

"What you talking Gus?" Cora snaps at Gus swangin' her head with hand on hip feeding off the gasps and pants from the gathering crowd.

"Just what I said, you ain't gotta worry 'bout Barbara or these boys, this here my family, they here to be with me."

"You ain't raisin my boys!" I yell as I jump in my brother's face loosening up my tie ready to go a couple rounds right here in church.

"Oh, now you ready to fight for your family. A few years ago you left them for dead. I spent more time with them boys than you ever did. You don't know one thing about them chaps. Barbara's mine, this is my family and now you can go on with the family you chose to be with."

"Pay him no mind Gus; you know what the bible says about a double minded man. Let's go to your sisters eatery I been hearing so much about, heard the cat fish is to *die* for."

Gus and Barbara exit with kids in tow and I follow out behind them. Gus chases away the few people that were waiting at his car to purchase one of his albums something he wouldn't do under normal situations. He loads up the children and speeds off from the church. Thomas, J.C, Bobby and Joseph laugh uncontrollably saying it's the funniest stuff they'd seen in a long time. Daisy, Delilah and Mabel had run over to help Cora who by this time has passed out after I tried to fight Gus over my boys. I see my mama and her proud parent look of earlier had turned to a look of disgrace. I storm out of the sanctuary seeking refuge in my study ignoring the knocks from the jacklegs and deacons pleading for me to open the door so they could pray with me. I didn't' respond. How could all this happened on today of all days. I cried out to Jehovah Shalom, and remembered it's all his will, and no matter how long and tearful the night will be, eventually joy will come with the morning…Whenever that may be.

DAISY

"What's good here Gus?"
Barbara asks her knight in shining armor as they enjoy the best seat in the restaurant, and I wait to get their order.

"Er'thang good here. Gone head get what you want, get you two or three different meals if you like, they's all gone be good."

Gus answers her, complementing my food, feeling good and looking even better. He'd finally attained the success he'd been searching for. It wasn't through the Blues review, but Sook did play apart in his good fortune. The gospel label Sook started sky rocketed, partly due to Gus crossing over and bringing a large part of his fans with him. He knew the sinners had to have an album they listened to on Sunday mornings while they sobered up.

"Miss Daisy Mae the place is adorable, a mighty fine establishment."

"Why thank you Barbara."

"And please excuse my debut at the church with all the confusion, that wasn't my intention."

"Pay it no mind, that's all Cecil's mess, he needed to clean that up long ago."

"I pray all is well between the two." Barbara innocently remarks.

I could tell she was lying.

"Where my brother in law?"
Gus cuts in changing the subject.

"You know we ain't together. Been living apart for a couple months already, we just go places together so people don't be talking."
Gus apologizes and I could tell they both were sorry he even brought it up.

"How 'bout I order for you two, I'm sure you'll like what I choose."

Gus and Barbara agree. I place their order and bring out a round of sweet teas and join the family at the table. Gus was tappin' his foot to one of his original gospel songs flowing through the amplifying system I had installed, and he was singing along in parts. I'm very particular about the music played in my restaurants, but Gus was always guaranteed to be on the play list secular or gospel.

"So Barbara, how long you had Nathalia?"

"Her mama came round to y'all Louisiana home looking for signs of Mah May bout a year ago. Said she didn't want the child no more, couldn't take it. Said the girl was fass beyond her years, messin' with grown men, ruint, no more good, even broke up her marriage. Said she was leaving her there with me and if I didn't want her then send her on her way, but she didn't want nothing else to do with the child."

"That's horrible, so what's your plan now?"

"I guess she mine?"

"You say that like she a thing, an object, a purse or something."

"Might as well be, I have to carry her around as such, what you want her?"

Barbara caught me off guard with her question. I look over to the other table and I see my brother in the beautiful girl's features. This was my niece who people have seemed to give up on. But not me, I will accept the challenge, others may have cowered away from the task, but I'm gonna do this.

"Sure. It'll be fun, we'll be help for each other, and I'm sure we'll both learn a lot."

"Hallelujah!!"
Barbara yells taking a big swig of her sweet tea; I sense she could stand for something a little bit stronger.

"Well baby you know what that means? We could move to Chicago like Sook been begging me to do. We could get away from all this madness and start over, as a family, no more ducking and hiding our love for each other!"

"You mean it Gus, baby I would follow you anywhere!"

"Dinners on me!"
Gus shouts as he stands on the top of his chair and the place goes wild. He asked the maître'd to put on his latest single and crank it up. The place was lively and Gus was on top of the world. I look at everyone enjoying themselves having a good time then I see Nathalia sitting there looking so alone, like her problems were flooding her mind and she was in a room all by herself. For a second I feel sorry for her, then I feel sorry for myself once I realize that her problems aren't only hers any more, they're ours.

18 JOSEPH

"Joe you spoil me, I love my new apartment."

"I love you, and there's nothing I wouldn't do for you. Besides, those hotels were getting too expensive."

"You woulda kept paying for them if you had to, ain't I worth it?"

"You're more than worth it Mabel, but now we can be together whenever we want and when you get better we could get a place big enough for the kids too."

"I don't know if the family is ready for us. I'm not quite fine with it yet, remember it took me forever to finally give in to us having our hide-a-way."

"But eventually you did, just like they will. Me and Daisy are through, been over for close to two years now. I'll always have love for her, she's the mother of my children but I'm in love with you. I want to marry you Mabel, I want you to have my baby. I recall the first day I met you, I was taken by you then, but I was so scared because you seemed so much more advanced than me. So I went with a safe choice, because I knew Daisy didn't have near as much life experience as me. But I can't hide it no more; I love you and have always loved you."

"Oh Joseph."

I lean in to kiss my lover and she begins to hack and cough uncontrollably which has been happening more frequently as her illness progresses. I pour her a glass of water from the pitcher on the night stand and by the time I turn around Mabel was passed out gurgling on blood. I roll her on her side to open her passageway as I call the paramedics. I rode with her as they rushed her to the Medical Center not caring how Mable will react once she becomes conscious. Of the many times Mabeleen had been admitted in the hospital over the past couple of years, she never allowed me to visit her for fear of what her family might say. If she knew I was about to check her into the hospital she would die; I'm doing it so she won't. After they take Mable to prep her for surgery, I call Mah May and tell her they to come right away. She didn't ask how I knew or what I was doing here, only said, "Thank you." I suspect May knew 'bout me and Mabel for a while now and I knew this could get messy but there is was no way I am leaving this hospital or my baby's side. J.C was the first Thomas to arrive, followed by Delilah and Bobby. Bobby said little to me, once thinking, but now knowing, me and Mabel had been sneaking around all this time. Little was said, we were all just waiting to hear from the doctor, but once Mah May and Daisy arrived the scene turned tense. Everyone was on edge, snapping at each other, and asking me questions I didn't have answers to. Finally when I see Cecil walk in, I think to myself, now things will simmer down since a man of God has arrived, oh, but how wrong I was. Once he was filled in on all the details, he had questions of his own.

"Joseph, how you come to bring Mabel to the hospital?"

"I tell you how," Daisy jumps in, "He sleeping with her, been doing it for some time now! Even shackin' up wit her in some lil' ol sin nest and left all dem children with mama!"

Once Daisy said that all hell breaks loose, J.C attacks me with a combination of rights and lefts and even though I was wrong in this situation, I was gone defend myself, and I did. We fought right there in the third floor lobby of the Medical Center. Delilah was hitting me with her purse and telling me how Bobby was gone whip my ass. Bobby said nothing, he was too busy trying to be peacemaker between me and J. C, but we were way past that. May was the only one who saw the doctor enter the room accompanied by security. They were about to throw us out but we were able to gain our composure before round two could start.

"Y'all need to get a hold of yourselves. Your sisters in there fighting for her life and y'all fighting each other. I know we all hurt, but Mabel is hurting more. We don't even know what's going on, but what we do know is that she has been ill for a long time. So think about your sister right now and not your selves.

"Doctor, whas wrong with my baby."

"Well ma'am, you daughter is very ill. It's a number of things, but one of our main concerns right now is her lack of kidney function. A transplant wouldn't be an option due to poor lifestyles choices she'd made through the years and dialysis would only buy her some time. There are alternative methods we could try, but they are quite expensive."

"Money's not a problem sir." May advise the doctor.

"Well Mrs., sorry I didn't get your name…"

"Thomas, May Thomas."

The doctor looks us over for the first time seeing our attire and accessories and realizes we weren't your average Negro family.

"Thomas as in Thomas Construction Company and Thomas Thomas, Los Angeles' first-round draft pick?" May didn't have to answer because just then Tommy arrived and came running over to comfort his mother.

"Well I guess money wouldn't be a problem." The doctor mumbles.
"We'll get her going on the new medication and set up a dialysis machine in her home once she's released. We'll provide full time nursing assistance also. Remember this is only buying her some time. Uhh... Thomas, do you think I could get your autograph, I'm a real big fan."

"Doctor you save my sister's life, there won't be nothing you can't have."

And with that the doctor left and so did all the negativity and anger. It had all gotten real. Mabel wasn't guaranteed much time with us and all our money couldn't save her. After that day, I don't know if the family really accepted me and Mabel as a couple, or just never said anything else against us within our earshot, but we never heard rumblings of our relationship again. By the end of the evening Mah May had us all singing and praying putting our souls in a better place. She never did things just to do them, everything was a lesson, and what she was trying to teach us today was that when praises go up, blessings come down.

MAH MAY

"Where's my grandbaby Nathalia, Daisy?"

"She went to send Watson a telegram updating him on Mabel's health. You know that boy always worrying 'bout his mama even when she wasn't sick."

"I bet Mabel didn't know she was bringing out the revolutionary in that boy by talking 'bout white folks over his head all dem years."

"I know mama, who woulda thought one of us would voluntarily leave California to go back south. At least it's for a good cause though, him doing sit-in's and freedom rides, Thanks to Joseph and his money."

"Speaking of Joseph, I never asked you how you was taking him and your sista being together. We kinda just swept it under the rug, never really talked about."

"Mama I'm fine. We been apart for a couple years now, it's okay. I got more male friends than I care to have, but I chose to focus on my children, my niece, and my career."

"Thas what mama wanna hear, cause when she have that baby, we all gone need to pitch in."

"Baby?"

"Oh I'm sorry sugar, didn't you know?"

"Naw mama, I thought her organs were shutting down wit everythang else, not working."

"Chile you know Mabel a baby making machine, she gone pump dem babies out through hell or high water."

"Well I's happy for them. It's for the best. I need to start my life over anyway and what better time than the present. Thomas has a friend he wants me to meet, says he plays football for the Chicago team, and wants me to come visit in the off season."

"See, thas good baby and at least you know he don't want none of your money, he got his own. So why not go meet him when we come from Thomas' last game in San Francisco? The season will be over, you can go see your brother and most importantly you need a vacation."

"I think I will mah, I think I will."

"Thas my baby."

Daisy loads up her children and drive down the long drive way to the traffic out on the street. I didn't mean to break the news to Daisy about the baby, but she needed to know. She's a beautiful girl and will have no problem finding a mate. Thomas looked out for her as he had the entire family. He bought me a brand new house just as he'd promised, even had J.C build it from the ground. He was always taking Daisy traveling with him, wanting her to find a companion. But all things take time and if she could get over her sister bearing the child of her ex-husband, then she'll be able to get over anything.

19 GUS

"Gus! Gus!"

I can hear Barbara calling me, but my body won't move and honestly I don't want it to.

"I'm tired of this shit Gus, you stayin' drunk and loaded all day and night. Got drugs on my table and my house reeking of alcohol. All you do is bring home the bacon and steal it back when I'm not looking. Ain't even good for sex no more!"

I knew eventually I was gone have to deal with this shit, might as well get it over with. Little does she know I'm tired of shit too, tired of the fact I can't get high in peace. I sit up and take a swig from the hair of the dog that bit me.

"What kind of example is you setting for your kids? You doing all this and supposed to be a gospel singer."

"What you mean *supposed* to be? I am a gospel singer, one of *the* best; I just do a lil' sinnin' in my off time." I inform my curious wife, as I fire up the magic and chase it with last night's bourbon.

"I'm tired Gus, you losing yo' mind. Staying out all times of the night getting high, singing in folk's church on Sunday mornings then demanding pay before service even over."

"How else was we gone afford all this shit you wanted? Fancy cars, home, furs you wanted all these thangs…how you 'spect I was to pay for it?"

"Your sisters in town, did you remember that Gus? Been here for weeks and you ain't went to see her once. She went to the studio and Sook told her he been let you go because of yo' drankin and druggin."

"Forget Sook, he don't understand artists, we a different breed, besides that man in Detroit heard I wasn't with Sooktown records no more and wants me to go secular."

"You can't go back! You have gospel fans! What they gone say?"

"Look here woman, 'they' ain't gotta pay all these bills, 'they' ain't gotta keep the magic coming. I gotta do that, and I intends on doing it, any way I know how. I made it out of Louisiana and got a name for myself and I'm gonna keep it that way…..'*oh that way*'…sounds like a hit."

I grab a pencil and paper and jot down what would be lyrics to my next single. I was known for pulling a song out my ass and making it number one on the charts. I could make a hit record out of thin air, and I was on to something with this one.

"Boy what wrong wit ya?"
Daisy bursts in tossing her fur stole and pocketbook down rushing up in my face.

"Have you lost your cotton pickin' mind?"

"Hey sis, just doing a little writing."

"Look like you doing more drankin than writing."

"I'm an artist, helps me with my ideas."

"Well you need to get yo' shit together, sister not doing well at all. Mabel don't have long and mama wants us all home."

I couldn't believe what I was hearing. I even sobered up long enough to hear the details about my sister. Daisy told me about the pregnancy and Joseph. She said mama told her at this point it was Mabel or the baby to survive. It was all so overwhelming, I felt so sad and scared for my sister. I turn the bourbon bottle down my throat and light the magic back up bringing Daisy to tears but at this point I didn't give a shit. Daisy left a plane ticket and told me to meet her tomorrow at the airport if I was going to see Mabel, and if I chose not to come, don't ever speak to her again.

20 CECIL

The mood in hospital waiting room is quiet and solemn even though we're all packed in here like sardines. Over the past few years we've been gathering here so often, the staff knows us by name, even gave us our own little waiting room anytime Mabel had to be admitted so we could visit her in comfort. We decided as a family that anytime our sister was to be in the hospital for a long period of time we would take shifts staying with her so she would never be alone. Mama came up with the idea, and I think it's something she decided to do after Nathaniel had to suffer and die by himself, I don't think mama ever got over that. No one said a word but had a lot to say. Everyone had their own opinion of who should live between Mabel and the baby. Mah May felt Mabel was grown, and had lived her life and if it came to a decision she was going to spare the newborns life. Delilah and J.C felt Mabel should be saved since the baby hadn't lived a life, it would be as if the child was never born. The conversation was getting out of hand so Mah May just put her foot down and said if we have to choose, we're saving the baby and we will all pitch in to help raise the child. Once she did that she didn't want to hear anything else about it. Daisy and Gus just sat quietly to themselves not having an opinion one way or next about the situation. Over the course of the last year, we had been able to deal with Mabeleen's health issues because the doctor always told us they could keep her comfortable as they start her on some new medical procedure being worked on that would buy Mabel more time. Well today, I think we all knew the hour has arrived, today I just didn't feel hopeful as the other times we'd been here, something felt different. I look over at Gus who's been nodding off all day and I decide to go speak with him, Daisy had told me about Gus' addiction problems and even if she hadn't it was written all over his face. He looked horrible; skinny and unclean with a distant look in his eyes like no one was home. Before I could make my way over to my lost brother, Joseph walks in with Mabel's doctor, shakes his hand and then exits the room.

"How'd he get back there to see Mabel, he's not even family!"
Delilah rushes over to the doctor charging like a betrayed lover.

"I'm sorry ma'am but I'm going to need you to sit down." The doctor advises disregarding the comment Delilah just made.

"I'm not sitting anywhere, what's going on here? First you let that man back there with my sister then you tell me to sit down….I want to see my sister now!"

Delilah embarks on a tirade cussing and trying to argue with the doctor. We all attempt to calm her down as the doctor ignores the scene making his way over to sit with Mah May. Only a few seconds pass before we hear mama break down crying. At that moment we knew our sister's ticket had been punched and she was riding that Glory Train. We felt ashamed arguing over the Lords will. He had to remind us of who the ultimate decision maker is by leaving us with no decision to make. We all cry, holler, scream and cry some more. Even those of us who were trying to be strong and comfort others couldn't hold our composure long enough to be effective. It was only when Tommy asked the doctor his question that the room got under control.

"Doc, what about the baby?"
The room got so quiet that you could hear a rat pee on cotton while we awaited the doctor's response.

"Your niece is fine, we'll need to hold her for a couple of days for observation, but she'll be ready for Mr. Freeman to pick her up in about a week."

"Mr. Freeman? Why would he be picking the baby up? We dat baby's family."

Delilah snaps putting her grief aside once again giving way to anger.

"Well ma'am, not only is he the father of the newborn, but he's also Ms. Mabel's husband, the chaplain married them last night."

"Married? Oh hell naw! If he thinks he's getting away with this he has another thing coming! I'll have so many lawyers on his ass he won't be able to shit!" J.C yells through the tears and pain.

"Well Mr. Thomas, that may be what you have to do, you may want to file for temporary custody once the child is released until it's all sorted out. But the way things stand; it looks as if Mr. Freeman is the only living parent, and that's usually who the court will give the child to."

What did he say that for, it was like all religion was lost by the Thomas family in that moment. The threats and profanity flying around the waiting room was terrifying. The doctor had to make his escape in order to avoid Delilah's verbal attack, Daisy passes out just thinking of Joseph taking her baby niece from the family, and Mabel's children all running around still crying from the news of their mother's death. On top of all that Bobby, J.C and Thomas wanted to go find Joseph and kill 'em for even thinking he would get away with raising a

Thomas without their blessings. I look to my mother, and I could see her heart was heavy. She saw me staring at her for direction, wiped her tears and told me what she always told me when I would come running to her for help.

"Don't look at me, ain't nothing mama can do, you ain't a child no more. Now you must look to the hills from which cometh your strength."

At that moment I knew what I needed to do. I took all that anger and began praying like I'd never prayed before, whaling deep from my soul. My siblings join in and we all call on the Lord together through all our collective tears. When we finish, we still hurt, but are hopeful. We understand that as a Christian, sad times come, but there will soon be joy. I turn to Gus for him to sing us some spiritual healing to our souls and he was nowhere to be found. I hadn't paid attention to him through all the commotion and he musta slipped out after hearing the news about Mable. I whisper a prayer to myself as my others siblings curse his name. The boy been singing to the Lord for his lifetime, I pray he remembers that those weren't just songs he been singing.

21 Cecil

I woke this morning thinking 'bout my father and
Nate. I thought of how good God has been to my
family by only allowing deaths hand to caress us
up unto this point. But today as I sit in the pulpit of
Faith Foundation preparing to eulogize my sister, I
realize that no matter how many or few of times I
must deal with a loved one's transition, it's still
gonna hurt. I look out over the three or four
hundred people in attendance and realize that they
are here because they all loved Mabel in their own
way. My focus then falls on Mabel's children. The
motherless souls clearly sadden but bravely sitting
there in all white as if little angels rallying their
mother on to heaven. Before we marched in her
youngest Ray-Ray asked could he help hold the
casket but Tommy assured his nephew that his
uncles had this and we were honored to do it.
Apparently, that wasn't comforting enough for
Ray-Ray so he made us all promise we wouldn't
drop his mama. We all wanted to laugh, but tears
fell instead just thinking of how much this baby
loved his mama. The boy was right about one thing
though, we were going to need some help. So
Delilah asked her spouse and one of our cousins
from Chicago to join my brothers as being
pallbearers. The two remaining Thomas girls
comforted mama in their finest furs, jewelry, and

hundred-dollar hairdos. Yeah they were hurting, but made sure they looked good while going through. Watson made it back to California and was able to spend some time with Mable before she passed and bo-garted his way in to be the fifth pallbearer. After the eulogy, I'll join the gentlemen as the sixth and final soldier to have this honor bestowed upon us of carrying my sister to her final resting place. When I acted such a fool about being the one to lay my sister to rest I knew it was going to be one of the hardest things I would ever have to do in life, but I felt no other preacher would be able to lay her away like I could. I was not going to be ok with it any other way. I scan the congregation in between my silent prayers and meditations finding myself looking for two people I expect to be here but doesn't seem to have arrived yet. I woulda heard Gus as soon as he walked in 'cause he woulda been sangin' like a crazy man. I know how he mourn so it's clear he's not here yet. And some small part of me wanted Joseph to come and pay his respects but I don't think has the guts. I hadn't seen my baby bro Gus since the day Mabel died; it's been well over a week and mama been dragging 'round feeling like she lost two children that day at the hospital and not just one. The service up into this point has been heart wrenching but in a weird way uplifting. It's my time to speak and I'm drawing a blank. All I feel are the sweat pellets racing down my forehead and the rest of my body is totally numb. I grasp each side of the pulpit to make sure I don't fall 'cause I can't feel my legs. I know I have to gather myself 'cause I promised that I was gone make Mabel proud of me today. Everybody looking for me to make them feel better but I can't remember nothing I wrote. I thought I could do this, but I guess I was wrong until mama hit me with a, 'take ya time baby, take ya time,' and that's all I need coupled with a prayer for strength then the words came pouring out directly from the heart. I focused on all the good things Mabel had contributed to all our lives and pointed out her positive attributes and how those qualities have manifested in her children. I went on to urge everyone to find the strength and faith that Mabel had found within herself to enjoy life and for us all to do the same. My words are little comfort to Mabel's babies. The only thing they know is their mother is dead and no amount of condolences would make them be okay with that. I can't blame the children 'cause I don't know how I would act if it was my mama laying there and I'm a grown man. I sit down after my impromptu message and gesture for the funeral directors to commence with the viewing. All walks of life filed past Mabel showering her with tears, kisses and a bunch of remarks of how good she looked in her fur, jewels and fancy hair-do. Its half way through the third hour of the service and the last person to view Mabel has exited as we asked the ushers to escort everyone out in order to allow us to view our loved one in private. Good thing too because these babies are outta control and its taking all of us to try and be of some sort of comfort. It was another hour before we could pry the children away from Mabel's casket and get them into one of the five, white family cars, then load our precious cargo into the hearse for one final ride. The children refuse to exit the cars once we arrive at the cemetery and didn't as we commit Mabel to the ground. We gather flowers, hug and chit-chat for a while after the Internment trying to make this moment linger on as long as we could. But we all know it's no use, this pill will have to be swallowed sooner or later. I assist mama with getting back into the car and turn to take one last look at my sisters resting place and I see Joseph in the distance. I can't act like I see him or even acknowledge his presence while everyone is here, I gotta make sure all the cars leave 'cause I don't think I can stand to see Mabel's soldiers go to war today. Once everyone is out of sight I approach my brother-in-law twice over already deciding that I wasn't going to be confrontational, but instead be the bigger man and extend the olive branch, no matter how bad I want to beat him over the head with it.

"Hey Joseph." He doesn't respond. "Look Joseph, I just wanted to thank you for making my sister so

happy in the last years of her life. You even slowed her down, who woulda thought that was even possible."
I awkwardly chuckle not really knowing what to do.

"I got the baby."
Joe finally responds, but I'm not believing what I'm hearing.

"What you say?" I snap thinking being the bigger man is overrated.

"I went to the hospital this morning and picked up *my* baby. Named her after her mama, Mabeleen Maybell Freeman. We going back to Alabama in the morning to stay with my mama, she gone help me with the baby."

I couldn't believe what I was hearing. He couldn't be serious, this had to be some sick joke that I didn't find funny at all. My intention wasn't to come and fight Joseph, but it looks like things have changed. I start taking off my suit coat and loosening my tie ready to let out all this frustration on Joseph's face.

"I'm sorry Joe; I can't let you do that."

"Alright Cecil, What you gone do beat me? You gone kill me? You all act like I didn't love Mabel; I am this child's daddy. I know she was your sister, and the way we got together wasn't right in some people's eyes, but I loved and still love her. I'm not saying I didn't love Daisy, but Mabel understood me. Now you can pummel me and beat me til your knuckles bleed, but if you don't kill me, I will be on that train tomorrow morning …with my baby."

I drop my fighting stance and think about my two families. I thought how it *was* possible to be in love with two women, hell I had done it, and my father before me. Who was I to judge this man for having loved two of my sisters, how could he not, they were irresistibly smart and attractive.

"Joseph, I don't agree with you carrying my niece across the country, but you are her daddy and my brother-n-law, I will respect your decision."

"Thank You Cecil, I know this is hard for you. I'm sorry for any confusion I've ever caused but I would do it again, if I was able to see Mabel one more time. I had been asking Mabel to marry me for the past year and she refused worried about what her family would say. But when I asked her at the hospital, I wasn't taking no for an answer, I didn't care who knew, and I wasn't gone let her have one more child out of wedlock, this was also my way to let her know her child would always have a father in her life."

"Good luck Joseph, and you might wanna stay away for a spell, it's gonna take time for this wound to heal."

"Will do, by the way…I saw you brother standing out in front of the hole-in-the-wall in China Town, you might wanna go find em, he didn't look to good. He was out there begging for change, I gave him a twenty, but you know that wasn't gone get him too far."

And with that Joseph drove out of the cemetery and out of our lives. The conversation brought forth healing and acceptance for me. I no longer was I angry with my father, I now understand him more and the decisions he had made when I was a child. I'm not saying what he had done was right, but I know he was only doing what he felt he had to do at the time. The funeral was over, and so was one of the worst days of my life. The only good thing that came out of today was that I had a change of heart about my father as well as Joseph. I pray my family will be just as understanding but since Joseph has taken the baby back south, they really have no choice.

22 DELILAH

We had a large family and they all had come from
Mississippi, Louisiana, and Chicago to pay their
respects. Even one of the cousins who had gotten
away in the shootout way back when was here
justa drankin', laughin' and reminiscing about
Mabel. Maybe the rumors 'bout him being the
father of one of Mabel's kids are true, if so, she
took that one to the grave with her. We agreed to
hold the repast at May Mays new home that
Tommy had built for her and even with all of our
family and a few churchgoers, we still had plenty
of room in the mini-mansion. We feasted on
chicken, catfish, collards, homemade macaroni and
cheese, black eyed peas and any type of dessert
you could imagine all compliments of The
Delectable Daisy. As the night went on, the crowd
thinned out, and soon it was just mama and us
children, well her remaining living children minus
Augustus.

"Mama, me and Daisy gone stay the night with
you tonight, we don't want you to be here by
yourself."

"Chile, mama alright, I ain't never alone, I takes
the Lord with me everywhere I go."

"Please mama, we want to! We'll scatter the kids around the different bedrooms and we can sleep in here with you."

"You and Daisy sleep with me?"

Mah May laugh's but doesn't object, the king size bed was more than enough room for the three of us.

"Tommy, where you gone sleep?" Mama questions her overgrown baby like he's a tot.

"Mama don't worry 'bout me, I'm going with J.C, need to clear my head, I'll stay with him tonight."

"Lawd, he gone take my baby to that whorehouse." We all laugh, and it was welcomed considering the day's events.

"Not only whores comes there mama," J.C jokingly tries to explain. "I have respectable women over too."

Mama knew all her boys had a weakness for women, just like our daddy. And she knew it was nothing she could do about that itch. So she sent J.C and Tommy on their way but not before giving them a quick refresher course on caring for their tally-whacker. We got the children situated and

Cecil eventually left after talking mama half to sleep about some epiphany he had about daddy. I don't know if mama was playing possum on Cecil but as soon as he was out the door, mama got up and went to go bathe. This gave me and Daisy time to discuss entering mama in the upcoming Mother's Day pageant being put on by the City's mayor office. The winner would get a big write-up in the Sunday paper, two round-trip airplane tickets anywhere in California and a host of free services and gift certificates from the more exclusive businesses throughout town. We knew mama wouldn't like being paraded about like that, but this time she has no choice after everything she has been through we just want to let the world know how much we love our mama.

THOMAS

"Tommy, ya big brother gone find you some company for the night, we gone stop by the lodge and find us a couple of foxes." J.C informs me boppin' to some Redding.

"Man you know I'm the last person that needs help getting a woman, but thank you anyway. I don't

even be drinking like that, why you be going to these bars anyway, you don't drink at all?"
"You wanna know why? Because bars have women in there who do drink, helps the ladies loosen up, not that I need it of course. C'mom bro, I'll have one with you this time so we can toast to Mabel. Besides, it's off season, you can have a drink or two, on me."

I finally agree with my brother, but it didn't matter, he was gone still stop at the lodge. It was Friday, and on Friday nights the lodge opened up to non-members and partied 'til dawn. This was J.C's environment; he didn't drink or smoke, did nothing but chase the hell out some women. The parking lot was full so J.C parked his '65 convertible Chevy on the sidewalk near the entrance anxious to get inside and get to mingling. As we hop out we hear some commotion and watch as two men fight in the distance.

"You see them two junkies over there? They fighting over whatever's in that bag 'cause they won't let it go."
I stop and watch the show and J.C does the same; we weren't going to pass up the chance to enjoy a good scuffle. Just as the fight was getting going, one of the men knocks the other out cold and takes off running with the paper bag in hand.

"He hit that boy like Cassius!"
J.C cracks as we run over to help the defeated brawler.

I make it to the man first who was still on the ground but now he was clutching his stomach in pain. I roll him over and ask if he was alright, but in that moment it was me who wasn't okay.

"He took my stuff, my stash, stop him!"

"Gus?"

I knew good and well who this man rolling on the ground was, but didn't want to believe it. I don't even recognize my own brother. He was skinny, dirty and smelled of mildew and wouldn't stop talking about that paper bag.

"Gus get yo ass up fucking junkie"
J.C snaps snatching his twin up off the ground ready to put something on him worse than the beating he just got.

"Why you keep holding your damn stomach? That man hit you in yo face fool!"

"Brother, I'm sick, feels like I'm gone die. I needs my medicine…let me borrow a couple of dollars, I promise I pay you back, I need to get my medicine."

"I ain't giving you shit for no dope. That's not medicine its poison, look at yourself. You been here over two months and mama only seen you one time. Get him to the car."

I do as J.C instructs and throw my brother over my shoulder and get him to the Chevy. Gus begs and pleads for us to let him out of the car, but he knew that was not going to happened now. He finally realizes he's not getting out, and starts asking what was we gonna do with him and where was we taking him. Did he really have to ask?

23 MAH MAY

I lay awake in my bed thanking the Lord for the time he allowed me to have with my baby Mabel and I thank him for my two daughters asleep on either side of me. It was so much going on today I never got my quiet, one-on-one time with my Jesus so I'm taking advantage of the time I have now. I still don't know what I'm gone do with Mabel's children. Some want to live with Delilah and the others want to live with Daisy, but Watson told 'em they all coming to stay with him once he moves back here from the south. As I finally begin to nod off, resting in my Savior, I hear a soft knock on the door and its Thomas asking me to come downstairs into the kitchen. I knew something had to gone awry 'cause they was supposed to be staying at J.C's and here they are back at my house. Before I can even get my robe and slippers on, my nosy bodyguards had already woken up and beat me downstairs trying to see what was going on. My nerves were at their wits end, what the boys could possibly want at this time of the night, well technically morning. I was raising all kinda sayings by the time I made it down the stairs but still wondering what brought these boys back to my door at this ungodly hour, but when I stepped into the kitchen and see Augustus sitting at my good table scratching feverishly, I knew.

"Augustus!!" I sternly shout, "What wrong wit' ya boy? Been playin' with the devil huh? See what happens when you run around actin' like you on the Lords side, when you really dwellin' in the devils backyard. You cannot serve two Gods or straddle the fence, this is what happens; God will not be mocked!"

"But mama…"

"Don't but mama me; I don't even wanna hear it. Is you tryin' to kill yoself? Dat what you want?"

"Mama, sometimes I think I'm better off dead." My baby responds with a bowed head never making eye contact.

When he said that, there was nothing else for me to say. I ask Tommy to get his big brother some clothes to put on and he gone give me lip about Gus being too little to wear anything he has. I told him to get something from one of the kids, hell I didn't care at this point, just get him out my face and into some water. J.C volunteers to put his twin in the shower and to set up the cot in the garage for him to sleep. Thomas and J.C leave for what I hope is the remainder of the night 'cause I wouldn't be able to stomach another surprise. The boys did an excellent job of getting Gus cleaned up and finally, the house was quiet. I reclaim my spot between my bodyguards once again as they sleep their exhaustion away. I try to convince myself that I'm sleepy but my mind's running wild and I begin to entertain the many thoughts crammed up in there. This one particular thought keeps creeping to the front of my mental but I quickly tuck it away like I've been doing the past two months when it tries to take over. The thought invades my mind like an embarrassing obsession I don't want anyone to know about, but I can't stop thinking on it. I'm ashamed every time I realize I'm entertaining this thought, but its persistence has me feeling like I may have to address it head on. It hadn't been done in so long, and I wasn't even sure if it could still be done. I just pray I don't have to result to it. I'll sleep on it, put it in the Lords hands; *lay and leave*. As always, he'll tell me what to do.

The next morning I wake weak in my body but strong in the Lord with mind still stuck on Mabel. I thank the Lord before maneuvering past the body guards turned sleeping beauties and make my way downstairs to cook and old fashioned breakfast for all my children the father has blessed me to be left with. I know this is the second child to ride that train, but it never gets any easier. Throughout my lifetime I've had to watch some of my closest friends bury children of varying ages and no matter how old or how young the child was, my friends were never the same after. Losing a child is like losing a part of yourself, you become a different version of you. So knowing this, I continue to hold to God's unchanging hand for that allows me to be able to mourn my children in heaven while being present for the one's here on earth. As I start breakfast for the family, I call over to J.C's and tell the boys to come eat, I even call Bobby since everyone else was already here. I didn't wake Gus; I wanted him to sleep off whatever was wrong with him. The girls were still upstairs, they been whispering about some big secret all night, ain't no telling what those two got going on. The grandchildren ate corn flakes earlier and were out back playing waiting on their uncle Tommy to take them to some amusement park later. J.C and Tommy enter through the garage door just as I was finishing up the bacon, the last thing to be cooked before the eggs.

"Mornin' mama, we rushed right over once you said breakfast, you know we wasn't gone miss yo homemade biscuits."
J.C greets, kissing my cheek on one side while stealing a piece of the bacon on the other, he thank I ain't see.

"Y'all got Gus up? Where he at now? I thought that boy was gone be sleep for at least a week."

Tommy asks greeting me in the manner of J.C but I stop him before he could be successful.

"MY PURSE!! IT'S GONE!"

We hear Delilah yell from the bedroom; I shake my head and take a seat. The girls run downstairs talking about their purses were gone, mine included, and then all hell breaks loose. The sisters start to run to the garage, and I tell 'em Thomas said Gus ain't out there but they went to look anyway returning with a look of utter disbelief on their face. Delilah became hysterical and poor Bobby could barely contain her.

"Where he at damn junkie!" Delilah yells adding in some words I don't care to repeat. I knew where my child was alright. He wherever them purses at.

"I'm gone kill 'em! Stealing from my mama, he dead!" Thomas yells adding to the already chaotic scene.

I sit and watch Daisy and Delilah threaten to call the police and press charges on my baby, while my boys vow to kill him before the police could even have a chance to. Bobby, bless his heart, a peacemaker by nature, kept trying to tell Delilah that they could replace the stolen checks and credit cards, but she was not trying to hear anything he had to say. I see my children in an uproar and at that moment I knew what I needed to do. My children were hurting from the passing of their sister, and it was easier for them to turn that hurt into anger and direct it at Gus. Hurt people, hurt people and my babies weren't gone be at each other's throats trying to take a life I birthed, a life the Lord entrusted me with. They were talking about hurting my child, even killing him and that just wasn't a decision for them to make.

24 MAH MAY

I sit in my room and prepare for some Mother's Day contest the girls have entered me in. Normally I wouldn't be participating in something like this, but the girls wouldn't have it any other way. I don't care to have attention being brought on me in such a fashion, but I didn't want to hurt my daughter's feelings since they were so excited about the event. I put on a fancy dress that had been custom made for me and I was layered in expensive jewelry by the girls while they tell me that I was the mother of a lifetime whether I was named the winner today or not. I have been praying that I wouldn't win, because lately I've been feeling more like a failure rather than a mother to be proud of. It was hard enough to bury two children, but to have one live child running around, doing drugs and robbing innocent people, that was like a knife to my soul. The night Gus disappeared, not only had he stolen our purses, but he had also raided my jewelry box and taken trinkets my children had given over the years. Those things didn't matter much to me but my daughters were livid as they recount the value of each missing piece. It wasn't that I didn't care for my gifts, it was that the items were replaceable. But it was one thing Gus had taken from me that night which let me know he was out of control. The only piece of jewelry that I have cherished my entire adult life and have never missed a day in close to fifty years of laying my eyes upon. It was priceless; and even though Gus knew how I felt about it, he still took it. That was a problem and that was bothering me more than anything that he was doing. The fact he doesn't care about my feelings, and I'm his mother, lets me know he has no regard for anyone out there on them streets. We hadn't heard hide nor hair from Gus after the night of betrayal, only that he hadn't paid a loan shark he owed some money and the man had people out looking for him also. It was all getting to be too much for me to bear, I felt there was nothing I could do to keep my baby out of harm's way. I was able to talk the girls out of pressing charges on their brother, but it was a different story with my boys. J.C, Cecil and Thomas had everyone they knew looking for Gus, even had a reward out. They gave strict instructions for whoever found him to do whatever they needed to detain Gus short of killing the boy....they wanted to save that for themselves. For weeks my children have been talking about how Gus would pay for hurting me, the boys ensuring death would be the price, no matter how hard I plead with them to let this mess go. They knew superior court judges up and down the state of California, and felt the punishment they would receive, if any, would be light, but after all would be said and done everyone would know not to mess over the Thomas boys mama.

"You ready Mah May?" Delilah yells from downstairs, "The boys gone meet us there and Daisy's already out in the car, c'mon, we gone be late."

I don't respond; I'll get there when I'm there. I take one last look at myself in the mirror, and remark on how well I appear for a lady who's been up for the past three days. Last week I sent the grand-babies over to Delilah's to stay a spell, while I prepared for the unthinkable. It took me over twenty-four hours to decide if I would even do what I had vowed to never do again in my life. I didn't know if I could still do it, but I had to try. The thought of Gus killing someone or someone killing him, was unbearable. I hadn't prayed the Eternal Peace prayer in over forty years, back when I had prayed for my husband's return. I have the same faith today in the prayer and its powerful effect as I did back then. It's a shame that eternal peace can't be achieved here on earth while we are living, but by us being human, it's impossible. So a never ending nap will have to be the answer for my dear boy Gus. I know peace is only for moments, not a lifetime and my Gus needed more than that. I didn't know if I'd been successful in my efforts since times are so much different now than they were all those years ago, but one thing I stand on is my God is never changing and my faith is never wavering. Me not knowing if the spirits made it to Gus or not, is making it hard for me to get up and go get in that car, but I do. The girls would never forgive me if I miss this because of some Gus concerns but I needed to know something before I step foot in that building. My greatest fear is being named Mother of the Year with a lying, doping, thief, and possibly murderous son on the loose. My children tried over and over to tell me that the decisions Gus have made in his life has nothing to do with me, but I beg to differ. At this point I was tired and it would send me straight to the grave if Gus was to hurt or kill someone. The boy needed peace, eternal peace.

"Ladies we're almost there. Smile mah, you look beautiful."
Daisy compliments gazing at me through her rear view mirror.

"Y'all heard from Gus?"

"Mama, this your day. Don't be thinking 'bout no foolishness, it's Mother's Day. Like Daisy say, can we get a smile?" Delilah asks while primping me like a baby dolly.

I don't change my expression, no need. I wasn't smiling 'cause I wasn't happy. I had no business here at no Mother of the Year Awards with all these unanswered questions running through my mind about Augustus.

"Mama, Gus is only one person, all your children are very successful, so one slipped through the cracks, that's Gus' fault, not yours. So let's go in here, and mama can you please enjoy yourself?" Daisy advises knowing so little about why we don't throw people away. We'll see if she feel the same after them chaps she got get grown.

The girls escort me into the hall and up to my seat with the other nominated mothers. The venue is decorated beautifully with impeccably chosen pastels flowing throughout the building along with fine china and crystal place settings for all us ladies to compliment and enjoy. The other mothers in attendance are so talkative and lively as they enjoy the champagne brunch put on courtesy of The Delectable Daisy. Not me though. I don't eat at all, I only sip water sitting motionlessly during the meal; only being cordial when need be. Even as the mayor reads the essays sent in by the contestant's families, I don't move an inch. Whenever the time came for a contestant to be highlighted, the nominee appeared all puffed up and proud like they raised these kids on their own. Shameful, it's only by the grace of God we don't kill these babies 'fore they start walking. But when my turn comes, the girls catch my attention and motion for me to smile. I try my best to conjure up a piece of a smile, but can't. The buzz around town was that I was a shoe-in to win for raising such upstanding and charitable contributors to society; model citizens. Hump, if they only knew. None of my children were perfect, but none had ventured too far down paths they knew were dead-ends like Gus was doing. The mayor continues on about my family and their roles in the community while I earnestly try to enjoy the afternoon, but cant. I hold silent devotion with myself as my soul screams out to Jehovah deep within. All the effort put into this day by my children confirms they love me so much, but yet and still my heart is heavy. As the mayor announces my name declaring me the winner of this year's Mother's Day pageant, I'm relieved that I can finally get out of here and go home. Just as I began to stand to make my way up to the podium and accept this sham of an award, I see Thomas, J.C and Cecil enter through the back doors of the hall, and I pause. As the crowd stands and cheers, I stay in my chair to see if Gus would be coming through the doors next. The clapping became louder and the cheers gain momentum the longer I remained seated but I didn't care, I needed to see what I need to see. I keep my eyes fixated on the back doors for what seems to be an eternity when my attention is re-directed to an old but familiar scene replaying itself out before my very eyes. My big, boy Cecil boldly standing brandishing a strange look of complacency with tears streaming down his face, clutching my husband's priceless pocket watch. At that moment, I knew it was done. Augustus was finally at peace that was not of this world, but eternal peace. It was then and only then that I was able to smile, go forth, and accept my award for Mother of the Year.